# Hiding Edith

LIBRARY AND ARCHIVES CANADA CATALOGUING IN PUBLICATION

Kacer, Kathy, 1954-
Hiding Edith / by Kathy Kacer.

(A Holocaust remembrance book for young readers)
ISBN 1-897187-06-8

1. Schwalb, Edith--Juvenile literature. 2. Jewish children in the Holocaust--
France--Biography--Juvenile literature. I. Title. II. Series: Holocaust remembrance
book for young readers.

8/07   940.53
       Kac

DS135.F9S364 2006          940.53'18'092          C2006-900179-0

SGL 37109   $16.25

Copyright © 2006 by Kathy Kacer

Edited by Charis Wahl
Author photograph by Nicki Kagan
Cover and text design by Melissa Kaita

The views or opinions expressed in this book and the content in which the images are used do not necessarily reflect the views or policy of, nor imply approval or endorsement by, The United States Holocaust Memorial Museum.

Every effort has been made to trace copyright holders and to obtain their permission for the use of copyright material. The publisher apologizes for any errors or omissions and would be grateful if notified of any corrections that should be incorporated in future reprints or editions of this book.

Printed and bound in Canada

*Second Story Press gratefully acknowledges the support of the Ontario Arts Council and the Canada Council for the Arts for our publishing program. We acknowledge the financial support of the Government of Canada through the Book Publishing Industry Development Program.*

ONTARIO ARTS COUNCIL
CONSEIL DES ARTS DE L'ONTARIO

Canada Council    Conseil des Arts
for the Arts      du Canada

Published by
SECOND STORY PRESS
20 Maud Street, Suite 401
Toronto, Ontario, Canada
M5V 2M5

# Hiding Edith

### a true story

## by Kathy Kacer

## Second Story Press

# INTRODUCTION

In 1933, the Nazi party, led by Adolf Hitler, came to power in Germany. Hitler was a brutal dictator who believed that the German people belonged to a superior race. Therefore, his goal was to eliminate those people whom he considered "inferior," particularly the Jews. He also persecuted the Roma people (then called "Gypsies"), the disabled, and everyone who disagreed with him. His larger aim was to conquer Europe — and then the entire world.

He began his conquest by marching into Vienna, the capital of Austria, on March 12, 1938. In September 1939, Germany invaded Poland and World War II began. Before the war, Jewish communities across Europe had been strong in numbers and spirit. There were many Jewish schools, libraries, synagogues, and museums. Jewish people played an important role in the cultural life of every European country, as composers, writers, athletes, and scientists. But the war brought rules and restrictions for Jewish citizens. Jewish land was confiscated, Jews were not allowed to attend universities and colleges, were excluded from most professions, and were forced to wear the yellow Star of David on their clothing. Jews were assaulted, arrested, and their businesses taken away. Later they would be sent to prisons and concentration camps to be slave labor; there they would be starved, tortured, and killed. By the time World War II ended in 1945, it is estimated that more than six million Jewish people died or were killed at the hands of Adolf Hitler and his Nazi armies.

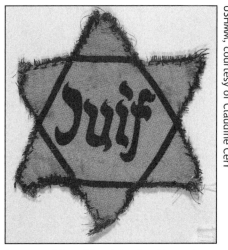

A star of David with the French word for Jew (Juif) printed on it.

As the war was closing in on Jewish people across Europe, many frantically fled from one country to another, trying to escape from Adolf Hitler's persecution, and trying to find a place where they might be safe. When Germany invaded northern France, some Jews sought refuge in the southern part of that country, which was known as a "free zone." The town of Vichy in southern France was the location of the free zone's government, under the leadership of Marshall Henri Phillipe Pétain.

The Vichy government wanted to have a good relationship with Adolf Hitler, and collaborated closely with Nazi Germany, hoping for favorable treatment in return. The Vichy regime actively persecuted Jewish people. Jews who had fled to southern France for safety were

Henri Phillipe Pétain

arrested and turned over to the Nazis to be sent to concentration camps. Over 75,000 Jews living in southern France were sent to the concentration camps. Of these, only about 2,500 survived the war.

As Hitler's forces invaded country after country, terrorizing the inhabitants and searching out Jews, safe places were few. Jews became desperate, fearing for their children's safety and their own. Many parents were forced to make a heartbreaking decision: to find someone to hide their children.

Jewish children were hidden in convents, on remote farms, in boarding schools and orphanages. Many Christian families were brave enough to take Jewish children into their own homes, even at the risk of their lives.

This was a different kind of hiding. Often the Jewish children lived openly, by concealing their identities behind new names and made-up histories — where they were born, how many siblings they had, who their parents were, even what language they had first spoken. They had to be watchful every moment, taking care with whom they made friends and how they answered even the most harmless-seeming question. Many attended church, hiding their Jewish faith, learning unfamiliar customs and rituals. Always fearful, always ready to move on if danger threatened, they would stay alive only as long as they kept up their disguises.

Thousands of Jewish children survived by hiding in this way. One was Edith Schwalb. Constantly afraid, she moved from place to place, concealing her identity and hiding her faith. This is her remarkable story.

Edith Schwalb

# CHAPTER 1

## May 1938
## Vienna, Austria

"Walk quickly, Edith," Papa urged. "Your mother will be waiting for us with a hot lunch. We don't want to be late, do we?"

Edith clutched her father's hand tightly. But Papa had such long steps that she almost had to run to keep up. She shifted her school bag and focused on avoiding the crowds of people surging around her. Men and women rushed in all directions, buzzing like giant bees. Cars honked their horns impatiently as pedestrians darted out into traffic. The sun beat down on Edith's head, and for a moment she longed to stop and savor its warm rays on her small face.

Vienna in May was alive with flowers and birds, smells and sounds. Cafés had opened their doors, inviting customers to come in and sit down. Street vendors paraded their wares: sweet ice cream and mouth-watering chocolate; other merchants displayed newspapers and magazines. Store windows were filled with colorful summer fashions. The city had woken up like a bear after its hibernation. And Edith wanted to take it all in. But she had to keep up with Papa, and that meant she couldn't stop.

The day was so beautiful and the city so energetic that Edith hardly even thought about how scary life was becoming. No matter how young you were, you couldn't live in Vienna in 1938 and not know that Austria was becoming dangerous. Two months earlier, Germany had invaded, and Nazi soldiers had marched right through the streets of Vienna. Austrian citizens came out to cheer, waving flags with the swastika, the emblem of the Nazi army, emblazoned on them. But Jewish families like Edith's did not cheer. They whispered the name of Adolf Hitler in fear. Hitler was the leader of Nazi Germany, and he hated Jewish people. He said that they were filthy, greedy, and dangerous. He said that Jews were the enemy of Germany and had to be stopped. He had promised that Austrian people would have a better life once they got rid of all the Jews. And now his supporters were in power in Austria, and wanted to punish anyone who was Jewish. They were stopping Jewish people from doing the things they normally did, like going to parks and playgrounds, and

A Nazi sign on a restaurant window in Vienna informing the public that Jews are not welcome.

even to some stores. Jewish businesses were forced to close or were being taken over by Nazi supporters.

Since the troubles started, Papa had come to get Edith every day after school, worried about her safety. Edith shook her head. She didn't want to think about that right now. Besides, she was hungry. School always made her hungry. Her stomach was grumbling, and she was dreaming about lunch.

"Hello, Herr Schwalb," a man called out, waving to Edith's father and interrupting her thoughts. "Wonderful game last night. Your last goal was most impressive."

Papa smiled and waved back but barely slowed his pace. Edith was accustomed to strangers stopping her father, shaking his hand, and even hugging him. His soccer skills were known throughout Vienna, a city that loved its sports — and its winning players. Papa hardly noticed the attention, but Edith loved it.

"There's the tram," cried Papa. "Come, Edith. Let's make a run for it."

He clutched his daughter's hand even tighter, and together Edith and her father sprinted across the busy intersection and jumped onto the open streetcar. Papa grabbed the railing just as the tram lurched forward. Edith nestled in under her father's big arm. She loved to stand on the streetcar just like this. With Papa holding on to her, she felt safe and secure, even as the streetcar bumped and swayed. The wind blew her short brown hair across her face, and she reached up to touch the white ribbon that her mother, Mutti, had tied in place that morning.

A streetcar adorned with swastikas, the emblem of the Nazi army, and a large sign announcing a meeting to support the takeover of Austria.

USHMM, courtesy of National Archives and Records Administration, College Park

"Engerthstrasse!" the conductor shouted moments later. "Watch your step as you descend."

Papa jumped down easily and turned to catch his daughter. Edith smiled as she grabbed her father's hand, and hopped lightly onto the sidewalk. *Only one block to walk and then I can eat*, she thought.

It was her last thought before the soldiers surrounded them.

"Gestapo! Papers, please."

A tall grim man stepped in front of Edith and her father, holding out his hand. Edith froze. She knew about the Gestapo. They were the special police force that carried out Hitler's orders, known for their cruelty to Jews. Just a week earlier, a Gestapo officer had beaten up her friend's father on his way home from work.

"My father was just walking along, minding his own business," her friend, Marta, had said. "But when they asked for his papers and saw that he was Jewish, they punched him hard in the stomach and left him lying on the road."

Edith thought about Marta's father as Papa calmly reached into the pocket of his suit jacket and pulled out his identification documents.

The officer grabbed the papers, glaring at the huge *J* on the first page. He barely glanced at Edith and her father. "Juden! Jews!" he muttered.

"Is there a problem, sir?" asked Papa, removing his hat courteously and addressing the Gestapo officer.

For the first time, the man looked up. His face showed such disgust! Edith had never seen so much hatred before, and it frightened

Jews are forced to scrub the pavement in Austria as Nazi soldiers look on.

USHMM, courtesy of National Archives and Records Administration, College Park

her. But as the man considered her father, his expression suddenly changed. Loathing turned to surprise and then to recognition.

"Herr Schwalb!" he cried. "I didn't recognize you. It's me, Ernst. We have played soccer together. I'm a big fan." The man was smiling now.

Papa remained impassive. "What is going on here, Ernst? Is there a problem?"

A sign on the front of a Jewish business in Vienna which reads "Not one penny to the Jews."

Ernst pointed off to one side of the street. An old bearded man and his wife huddled together, along with several other people, surrounded by soldiers guarding them with guns. "It's a roundup," he said. "We are arresting Jews for questioning. We'll rough them up a bit before we send them home — teach them a lesson." There was a girl Edith's age in the group, and for a moment, their eyes met. The girl seemed terrified and helpless. Edith quickly turned away. Ernst was peering at their papers. Then he straightened and looked around. When it appeared that no one was watching, he leaned in and lowered his voice.

"Get out of Vienna, Herr Schwalb," he whispered to Edith's father.

"I don't understa—" Papa began.

"Get out now!" With that, the officer pushed the documents into Papa's hands. "Gestapo! Papers, please," he bellowed to the people next in line. Edith and her father quickly moved off.

"Papa, what did that man mean?" Edith asked when she and her father were out of earshot. "What are we supposed to do?"

"Quiet!" her father replied with a brusqueness that startled Edith. Then he glanced down and placed his hand on his daughter's shoulder, smiling sadly. "I'm sorry, my darling," he said. "We'll talk when we get home."

∾

"There is no time to lose," said Papa, after he recounted

The sign on the telephone pole reads "Jews are not welcome here."

the incident to Edith's mother. "I say we pack now and leave. This instant."

"But how can we leave everything behind?" Mutti cried. "Our home, your business — it's impossible!"

"It's necessary," Papa urged. "Jewish families have been taken out of their homes. And who knows what has become of them." Papa moved closer to his wife. "We could have been arrested today, Magdalena. Edith and I are here only because Ernst recognized me. What good is my business if I'm in prison? What good is our house if we're not together as a family? We need to get out of here."

Edith stood in the hallway next to her sister, Therese, listening to their parents talking. "Are we really leaving here, Therese?" whispered Edith.

Therese placed her arm protectively around Edith's shoulder. "Don't worry, Edith," she replied, trying to sound confident. "Everything will be fine." Even though she was three years older than Edith, Therese looked very small and unsure.

Mutti appeared from the living room. "Come, girls," she said. "You heard your father. We have an adventure ahead of us. There is a lot to do and very little time."

Within two hours, Mutti had gathered clothing and food into small bags. Large suitcases would draw attention on the street. Edith and Therese helped, collecting their skirts, blouses, and sweaters for Mutti to pack. They moved quickly, barely speaking. Lunch was all but forgotten. The hunger pangs in Edith's stomach had disappeared, replaced with uncertainty and sadness.

Finally, they were ready. "Choose one thing from your room to take with you, Edith," Mutti said.

*One thing*, thought Edith, as she looked around her room for the last time. *One thing out of all my beautiful toys, books, and dresses.* She finally settled on a small doll she had had since she was born, a gift from her favorite uncle, David. The doll's name was Sophie. Her clothes were old and worn in places, and over the years, she had lost most of her hair; but she was still Edith's most special treasure.

The beautiful spring day had turned ugly, and Edith's heart felt cold and empty. She clutched Sophie tightly as the family walked away from their home, not knowing when or if they would ever return.

Edith and her family

# CHAPTER 2

*May 1940*
*Belgium*

The pounding on the door startled Edith out of her deep sleep. She pulled the blankets up to her chin and snuggled closer to Therese on the pullout couch they shared. Maybe the banging was just part of her dream. But seconds later, the pounding returned.

"Open the door," an angry voice barked.

This was no dream. Papa was at the door in a moment, clutching his housecoat around his pajamas and running a nervous hand through his tousled hair.

Mutti stood close behind him. "Don't answer," she whispered. But Papa took a deep breath and opened the door.

Three Belgian policemen in uniform entered the tiny apartment. Two carried guns. The third moved within inches of Papa. "Chaim Schwalb?" he demanded.

"Yes," replied Papa calmly. Even in the face of this obvious danger, Papa would not show fear.

Edith sat up in bed and rubbed her eyes, only to see Papa standing nose to nose with the police officer. "What is it you want, sir?" Papa was asking politely.

Edith's parents, Magdalena and Chaim Schwalb

"You're under arrest," the policeman barked. "We're taking all male Jews in for questioning." He spat the word *Jews* as if it was poison. "Five minutes to dress."

Papa nodded. It was almost as if he had been expecting this. He guided Mutti into the one small bedroom at the back of the apartment. Edith and Therese quickly followed and closed the door behind them.

"Don't worry," Papa said. "I'm sure this is nothing. I'll be back home soon." But he grabbed several sweaters, pulling them on one over the other as if he expected to be away for some time and wanted to make sure he could keep warm.

"We should have left," whispered Mutti. "When Hitler invaded Belgium, we should have known it would only be a matter of time before the soldiers came looking for Jews. It's just like Austria."

Edith squeezed her hands against her ears. She did not want to hear this. She did not want to feel so afraid again. The last time she had felt this fear was when her family had fled Vienna. It had taken more than a week for them to reach the Belgian border, a frantic journey of cars, trucks, and never-ending walks, mostly at night. They traveled mainly through the forest, venturing out onto roads to catch a ride with a passing farmer only when Papa knew it was safe. He always kept watch. Were they being followed? Did anyone suspect they were a Jewish family?

*How did Papa know where to go and whom to trust?* Edith never asked but watched silently as Papa would hand money to strange men, who then pointed in a vague direction. He would nod and the family would move on, Edith's jacket clunking against her hip with each step. Before leaving Vienna, Mutti had sewn a small bag into the jacket lining. She had put all their money in it, adding her pearl necklace, ruby ring, ivory brooch, and a few silver spoons. "We'll need money to live on, so take care of the jacket, Edith," Mutti had warned.

Mostly the family slept in deserted farm buildings during the day, emerging only after dark to continue their journey. But one day, Papa had not been able to find anywhere safe to sleep. The sun was already climbing in the sky: they had no choice but to ask for shelter. Edith and the others peered out from the woods as Papa knocked on the door of a small cottage, removed his hat, and spoke with the farmer. Then he motioned to Mutti. Wordlessly she reached inside Edith's jacket lining and gently pulled out the pearl necklace. Papa handed the necklace to the farmer, who motioned to the barn, then closed the door of the cottage. Carrying the family's valuables was a huge responsibility, which made Edith both proud and terrified.

As frightened as Edith felt during their journey, she had trusted Papa to keep the family safe. And he had. Until now. But as she watched her father gather a few belongings for prison, she felt a new, overwhelming fear. Edith glanced over at Therese, who was holding Gaston, her baby brother, born shortly after her family arrived in Brussels. Even he seemed to understand the gravity of their situation — his eyes were two round moons, his tiny hands clenched in tight fists.

"Hurry up, Jew!" The soldier called out. Mutti ran into the kitchen, grabbed some bread and salami, and pushed it into Papa's hands. "Take this. You must keep your strength up," she said. "I'll get you out, I promise." The soldiers laughed and pushed Papa out the door in front of them.

In the apartment, no one moved. Edith struggled to breathe. What was happening? Brussels was teeming with Jewish families like Edith's. It was supposed to be safe here. Life was supposed to be normal. And it had been. Edith and Therese had gone to school. Papa had found a job taking photographs of families for special occasions. It didn't pay much, but it was enough to buy food and cover the rent on their small apartment. Mutti, Papa, and Gaston slept in the tiny bedroom. Edith shared the pullout couch in the front room with Therese. They had all slept soundly — until the Nazis invaded Belgium, too. Then no Jews slept peacefully, and even Edith knew her family was once again in danger.

Mutti was running around the apartment, dressing and gathering more articles of clothing for Papa. Finally she reached under the couch mattress and pulled out a small bundle of money. When they moved into the apartment, the little bag of valuables had been taken out of the lining of Edith's jacket. "Now you don't need to carry it, Edith." Papa had said with a chuckle. "Now you can sleep on it!"

Mutti shoved the money into her purse. "I'll be back as soon as I can."

"What are you are going to do?" asked Therese.

Mutti shook her head. "I don't know, but money talks. I'll buy Papa's freedom." Her face had a determined expression. She kissed the children on the tops of their heads. The touch of her fingers lingered on Edith's cheeks. "Stay together, and stay inside," she said.

Edith, her parents,
Therese, and Gaston
in Belgium, 1940

"Therese, you're in charge." Then Mutti opened the door and left the apartment.

"What's going to happen, Therese?" Edith asked.

"Everything will be fine. Mutti is very clever. She will be able to do something." Therese was eleven, almost grown up, so she should know, thought Edith. But Therese had become so quiet in the past two years, so serious and withdrawn, that Edith was not sure that Mutti was going to be able to help Papa.

Edith planted herself by the door, listening for familiar steps on the staircase. "Come, Edith," pleaded Therese. "I'll make tea and we can read together." But Edith shook her head. When she finally heard the sound of the front door opening, Edith threw open the door and rushed into the hallway. It was Mutti — but she was alone.

"I'll try again tomorrow," Mutti announced. "We'll talk no more about it."

Edith tossed and turned for hours that night. When she finally drifted into sleep, she dreamed that her family was walking through the forest again. "Hurry up, Edith," Papa called through the dark night.

Those walks had felt endless, trudging through the forest and trying to keep up. Edith's jacket had bumped and banged against her legs in rhythm with her footsteps. "Papa, I'm so tired. My legs are aching," she had whimpered. Finally, when she felt she couldn't go another step, Papa had lifted her high onto his shoulders. She had clasped her hands under her father's chin and rested her cheek on his head.

Suddenly her dream changed. She was still in the forest, but now Nazi soldiers were closing in on the family. "Run, Edith!" Papa's voice was harsh and urgent. Her small legs throbbed, and her lungs felt as if they would explode. Papa dropped back between the family and the soldiers, pushing his family ahead in front of him. Edith turned to look back, but her father was nowhere in sight. *Papa! Papa!*

Edith sat bolt upright in bed. Sweat clung to her forehead, and her heart was pounding. Had she screamed out? She couldn't have — there was Therese, still sleeping. Yet the dream had felt so real! Papa had disappeared, and Edith had been alone. She took a deep breath. The dream was only a dream. Papa would come back. They must just wait. She had to believe that.

The family rose early in the morning, dressed, and ate a silent breakfast. Then Mutti left the apartment; Therese was to look after Edith and Gaston. Edith read with her sister and played quietly with Gaston, always anxiously watching the door, praying that when Mutti came home, Papa would be with her.

On the third day, Edith's prayers were answered.

"Papa!" Edith screamed, throwing herself into her father's arms. He reached down to hug the children. He was pale and tired.

"What happened to you, Papa?" demanded Edith. "Did the soldiers hurt you? Mutti, how did you get Papa out?" Her father just shook his head.

All Mutti would say was "I told you money talks. It's a good thing you kept ours safe, Edith."

Edith beamed, but her excitement did not last long. Papa gratefully accepted the tea that Therese handed him, and then announced, "We must leave Belgium. We'll go tomorrow."

Edith was not surprised. She knew that her father was lucky to be released. The family would have to disappear quickly, before someone came for him again.

"Where will we go?" asked Therese. "Are there any safe places for Jews?" Country after country had fallen to the Nazis, not just

Belgium but Poland, Hungary, Denmark, Spain, and Italy. Where could they go?

"France," said Papa." I learned from some men in prison that the Red Cross here in Brussels is helping Jews cross the border into France."

"The Nazis are already in Paris and the north, but in the south there is a free zone. It's safe there … so we've been told." Mutti lowered her eyes, trying to hide her uncertainty.

"We'll be fine," Papa said. "Haven't we been fine until now, thanks to your clever mutti?"

Edith looked away. She did not feel very fine. Her parents offered only empty reassurances. And she was tired of running. Besides, if Belgium had become unsafe, wouldn't it be the same in southern France?

"Come, everyone," Papa said. "We need to pack, and get some sleep. Tomorrow will be a long day." He leaned over to kiss Edith tenderly on both cheeks. He did the same with Therese and Gaston.

The last thing Mutti did that evening was remove the remaining valuables from beneath the couch mattress. They would once again be sewn into Edith's jacket.

Later that night, Edith climbed into bed. Her mind was racing. *Maybe France will be safe. Maybe we can stop running. Maybe the war will be over soon.* She yawned and snuggled closer to Therese. *Maybe Therese will smile again.*

# CHAPTER 3

## February 1943
## Beaumont-de-Lomagne, France

"Hurry up, Edith," Therese called impatiently. "Run! We're going to be late for school."

*People have been telling me to hurry up my whole life*, thought Edith, pretending not to listen. She was sick of running, first from Vienna, then from Belgium. When they came here to southern France two years ago, Mutti had called it a "free zone." But it wasn't really free. President Pétain thought he could get better treatment for his people by going along with Nazi policies and hounding the Jews. Jewish businesses and property had been handed over to the Nazis. Jews had lost their jobs and could no longer shop in many stores or be out on the streets after dark. Even so, the family had been safe here in the small town of Beaumont-de-Lomagne. But in late 1942 Hitler extended the occupation to southern France, and Jewish men began to be arrested.

Edith wondered for the millionth time about what had happened to her papa. All she knew was that he was gone. Soldiers had come pounding at their door late at night, just as they had in

Belgium. Mutti begged the soldiers not to take Papa; Therese and Edith trembled behind her, holding Gaston and sobbing. But the soldiers ignored Mutti's pleas, and Papa could only give her one quick hug before being led from the house.

"This is the last of my jewelry," Mutti had said, staring at the ring in her hand. Edith had long outgrown her jacket, but the family's valuables were still hidden in it. "The prison camp is close by. I'm going to try to get Papa released."

Edith sat by the door day after day, waiting for her father to come striding up the path, calling her name. But it never happened. Mutti returned each day, empty-handed and alone. Edith shook her head, trying to push that last sight of Papa from her mind. *I know Papa will come back,* she prayed. *I know we'll be together.*

"Edith, if you don't hurry up, I'm going to leave you behind!" called Therese.

"You can't!" Edith shouted back. "I'll tell Mutti."

"If I don't get to school on time, I won't be able to write the placement test to move up a grade. Please, Edith. I'll make your bed for a week. Just hurry up."

Sometimes Edith resented that Therese was such an excellent student. They had moved so often and missed so much work, yet Therese sailed through her classes, while Edith struggled so much that she didn't care about arriving at school on time.

"What do you want to be when you grow up, Therese? You're smart. Maybe you should be a lawyer or an engineer. Or be a teacher and make school more fun for students like me."

The two girls wound their way along the sloping hillside, through the narrow streets of Beaumont-de-Lomagne.

Therese brushed back her curly red hair. She had inherited it, and her fair, creamy skin, from Mutti; both made Edith envious. "What's the use of thinking about the future," Therese snapped. "We're just lucky that we can still go to school."

That was true. Edith knew that Jewish children elsewhere were not allowed an education. Still, Edith sighed. "You're so gloomy, Therese. I always think about what I'm going to be when the war is over."

"You must be joking, Edith. The war will never be over."

"How can you say that?

"Because it's true," snapped Therese. "Because nothing good has happened to us, and nothing will."

"I'm not listening to you," said Edith. "The war will end and Papa will come back."

"Stop it! Just stop babbling," commanded Therese. "You know perfectly well that Jews who are arrested are being sent to concentration camps. Mutti told us."

Edith turned away. She knew about the concentration camps, terrible places where prisoners could be tortured and killed.

"Face facts, Edith. That's probably where Papa is right now," Therese went on. "So just forget about the future. I'm tired of listening to your silly fantasies."

The cold wind blew through Edith's jacket and snatched the scarf from her head. How could Therese even think that Papa might not come home! And Edith wasn't a dreamer. She just couldn't give up hope. But Therese had stomped off to join her friend, Ida, who was a bit ahead on the path. Therese and Ida were talking in low voices, even though no one was around. Edith moved closer to listen in on their secret.

"Have you heard?" Ida asked. "There have been more arrests of Jews."

"But they've already taken all the men," whispered Therese. "Do you think they could come for us as well?"

"I don't know. But my mother isn't taking any more chances." Ida lowered her voice even further and Edith strained to hear. "I'm leaving."

"Leaving! Where to?" Edith shouted.

"Sh ..." Ida and Therese scowled.

"Where are you going?" This time Edith whispered.

"My mother knows of a place. It's in a town north of here, called Moissac. It's a house run by the Jewish Scouts of France, and it's supposed to be safe."

"But if things are dangerous here, won't they be just as dangerous there?" replied Therese.

Ida shook her head. "No. They've been taking in Jewish children for several years, and they know how to protect us."

"Who is *they?*" asked Edith.

"Shatta Simon and her husband, Bouli. They run the place. Listen, Therese," continued Ida, "your mother needs to go speak with

Jewish scouts from the Éclaireurs Israélites de France (Jewish Scouts of France) seated on a hillside. This is the organization that provided money for the house in Moissac.

USHMM, courtesy of Eytan Guinat

Shatta and find out more. But take my word for it, we need to do something or else we'll be in the next roundup."

Edith's head was spinning. She didn't want to run again. She wanted to stay in one place, and with her family. It was so crazy, having to run all the time just because they were Jewish.

Another cold blast of wind blew against Edith's face, and she pulled her scarf back up over her head. Therese took Edith's hand and squeezed it reassuringly.

"We're not going to have to leave again, are we, Therese?" asked Edith.

Therese took a deep breath. "Don't think about it now, Edith," she replied. "We'll talk to Mutti after school."

# CHAPTER 4

## The Decision

After dinner, Mutti announced her decision. To the girls' surprise, she already knew about the house in Moissac.

"I've been thinking about this for some time and trying to find a way to tell you," Mutti explained. "Perhaps it's good that you have found out about this safe house on your own. Since the arrests I've known that we would have to leave here and find a safer place."

Edith held her breath, not wanting to believe what she was hearing.

"Besides, there's no money left," Mutti continued, "and I have no way to care for all of us. Families in the next town have agreed to take Therese and me. You and Gaston will go to Moissac."

"But I don't want to go," cried Edith. Surely Mutti was not really thinking about sending her away. "I won't go, Mutti. Please tell me I can stay with you." Edith looked around, desperate, but Therese wouldn't meet her eyes. Gaston, listless and silent, sat idly drawing on a scrap of paper.

"I've tried to think of another way, Edith. But this is the best solution." Mutti was firm.

"But if we all leave, how will Papa know where we are when he comes back? We have to stay here and wait for him." Edith knew she was grasping at straws, but she was desperate to stay.

Mutti didn't respond.

"But why can't we just go somewhere else together?" Edith was not going to give up. "Or why can't Therese go to Moissac?"

Mutti stroked Edith's cheek. The years of running had worn Mutti down. Her beautiful face was drawn and tired. The twinkle that had always lit up her eyes had faded. "I have tried to find a place for all of us, Edith. Believe me, I've tried. But who will take a mother with three young children? No one! If people are caught helping Jews, they'll be arrested along with us. I'm lucky I found a house for Therese. She's old enough to work and pay her way."

"I can work, Mutti," Edith cried. "I'm strong, and fast. I can do anything Therese can do."

Mutti tried to hug her daughter, but Edith pushed her away.

"You don't love me!" Edith shouted. "You love Therese more than me. That's why she's staying with you. That's why you're sending me away. Papa wouldn't send me away."

Edith sobbed and thrashed wildly at her mother. Mutti grabbed Edith's arms and gradually gathered her in a warm hug. Edith's weeping turned to soft whimpers and then to silence as Mutti rocked her.

"I'm doing this *because* I love you so much," Mutti whispered as she stroked Edith's hair. "I wish your papa were here, too. I wish everything was different. But believe me, I am trying to do what's best for all of us. I'll go with you and Gaston to the house in Moissac as soon as plans are in place."

# CHAPTER 5

## March 1943
## Leaving Mutti

"Everyone here in Moissac knows we're Jewish. The whole town keeps our secret safe!"

Edith couldn't believe her ears. Even Gaston, sitting next to her, clutching his small bag of clothing, seemed to understand that something astonishing was being said.

"Please, Madame Simon," said Mutti. "Explain to me again how it is that you protect the children."

"Call me Shatta. Everyone does. We are a family here," the director responded warmly. "We've been protecting Jewish children in this house since 1939, and in other houses like ours across France. Our children come from many different countries — France, Belgium, even Germany. They have all been separated from their parents. So you see, Edith, my dear. You are not alone."

Edith was not sure she liked being called "dear" by this stranger, seated behind the large wooden desk. Shatta Simon was a young woman in her early thirties. She had dark wavy hair and dark eyes. She was large and rather imposing; but she had a kind smile, so Edith was not afraid.

"Children have come to us when their parents were taken away — to prison or a concentration camp. In many cases, we don't know what has happened to their parents. Or parents like you, Mrs. Schwalb, who fear arrest, have brought their children here to be safe."

Edith turned away. It was bad enough that Papa had been taken away. She could not bear the thought that Mutti might also be arrested. Besides, Mutti was coming back for her. She had to.

"We receive money from the Jewish Scouts of France," continued Shatta, "and we follow the philosophy of the scouting movement: be prepared, and help your neighbor."

Edith didn't know much about the Scouts. There were Scouts in Austria but they were even older than Therese. And she'd never heard of Jewish Scouts.

"In spite of what the Nazis are doing, the Jewish Scouts is a strong organization," Shatta continued. "Without their help, we would not be able to manage. But perhaps more important, we have established good relations with the people of Moissac." Shatta leaned forward and smiled at Edith. "The mayor is our friend. He protects us, as do the townspeople."

Was this possible? Were the people of Moissac, even the mayor, risking their lives to help their Jewish neighbors? This was amazing — most people were too afraid to help Jews. Should Edith feel relieved, or worry that Shatta wasn't telling the truth?

"You'll have to trust me on this," Shatta continued, as if reading Edith's mind. But Edith didn't know whom to trust: Mutti was sending her away, which felt like the biggest betrayal of all. And Shatta was a complete stranger, who had told the children's secret to all the other strangers in this town. Could they be trusted? Would even the children of Moissac not tell? Nothing was making sense.

"Come, Edith, Gaston," Shatta said. "It's time to say goodbye. Our staff will take you to your rooms."

Gaston clung to Mutti's neck, trying not to cry as she whispered in his ear and stroked his head. Then Mutti kissed Edith on both cheeks. "I will visit you when I can," she said, trying to keep her voice steady. "Be a good girl."

Edith could not say a word; there was nothing to say. She dissolved in tears in her mother's arms. Her head understood why Mutti was leaving her, but her heart was breaking. Finally, Mutti gently pulled away and looked deeply into Edith's eyes. "Remember who you are," she said. And then she was gone.

The library
at Moissac

Edith rubbed at her tears with the back of her hand; she did not want Shatta to see her crying. She had to be strong. But Shatta had watched these goodbyes more times than she could count. She understood how painful it was, both for the children and for their parents. She handed Edith a handkerchief, saying, "It will take time for you to get used to being with us, Edith. I'm not going to pretend that it will be easy. But our children become strong in our care, like strong Scouts. You will be safe here, and you will adjust. And I hope you will make the best of it." And with that, Shatta led Edith out the door.

Shatta and Bouli Simon

# CHAPTER 6
## Meeting Sarah

Edith carried her small suitcase and followed Shatta up the stairs, down a long hallway, and into a large bright dormitory with ten beds facing one another in two neat rows.

"This will be yours," Shatta said, pointing to a bed close to the window. "Unpack your things and put them on this shelf. The girls are in evening activities, but they will be back shortly. The toilet and shower room are down the hall. If there is anything you need, I'll be in my office. Otherwise, sleep well, Edith. I'll see you in the morning."

Edith sank down on her bed. She bit her trembling lip but didn't cry. She had cried so much in the past few days that it was almost as if she had no more tears left.

She pulled her suitcase onto the bed and opened it. It was times like this when Edith longed for Sophie, but her doll had been lost during one of the family's many moves. Mutti offered to buy Edith another doll, but it wouldn't be the same. Besides, Edith still found comfort in talking to Sophie.

"You're the only one who knows how I really feel," Edith said softly, as she pictured herself hugging her doll tightly. "I'm scared, Sophie. There's no one I can talk to, and no one who remembers with me." She closed her eyes, trying to remember Vienna and Papa waiting for her after school. She struggled to conjure up her father's face and the special smile he reserved just for her. She longed to be back in Brussels, or even Beaumont-de-Lomagne, reading stories with Therese or listening to the music that Mutti played on the record player. She tried making bits of memories into pictures: what did Papa look like in his soccer uniform? What did Mutti's dress look like — the one she used to wear to the opera? What were the names of all her dolls? But the connections were too fragile and broke like worn thread.

Edith had just placed her sweater on the shelf when she heard voices approaching and footsteps racing toward the room. A group of girls sprinted through the doorway, giggling and shoving one another playfully. They stopped when they saw Edith.

"Hello." A girl approached Edith and held out her hand. Edith shook it solemnly. "My name is Sarah Kupfer," the girl said. "You must be Edith Schwalb. Shatta told us that you were arriving today. You've got the bed next to mine." Sarah had pretty blue eyes and long blond braids. She also had a warm and friendly smile. Edith was relieved that the girls knew who she was, as one by one they introduced themselves. They seemed friendly, which was a relief; they even seemed happy. It didn't make sense: all these girls had been separated from their families, yet they seemed so cheerful!

"I don't know where my mother is," Sarah said, as she helped Edith push her suitcase under the bed. "She's gone into hiding with my brother, somewhere east. My father was taken away. We don't know where."

"That's almost exactly like my family!" Edith exclaimed. "Except it's my sister who's with my mother. My little brother is here."

Sarah nodded. "Everyone's story is the same — or almost. That's what makes us a family here."

"That's just what Shatta said."

"Shatta's wonderful," said Sarah enthusiastically. "She's quite strict, kind of like a general keeping us all in line. But she's very kind, and very smart. She runs this place and organizes all the activities. Wait until you meet her husband, Bouli. He's like everyone's father. But be careful — he's going to want to put drops in your nose to keep the germs away." Sarah wrinkled up her nose and laughed. "And when you're eating, if he sees your elbows on the table, he'll bang the table to teach you manners. But don't worry," she added quickly, noting the frightened look on Edith's face. "He's really very sweet."

Several girls began to sing in another corner of the room, their voices blending sweetly. "We have a choir here," Sarah continued. "You'll meet Henri, the choir director. He'll want you to join. And you'll also meet Germaine, our counselor."

Edith paused. "Everyone seems so … so happy," she said. "How's that possible?"

"None of us laughed when we first arrived," replied Sarah. "I cried myself to sleep for a week. But think of what's out there! This is the best place you could be."

Edith nodded. Out there were arrests, restrictions, prisons, and people who hated her. But could it really be different here? Was Moissac really untouched by the war?

"Did Shatta tell you that the people in Moissac know we're Jewish?" asked Sarah. "Everyone — children, grown-ups and all the town officials. Can you believe it? If the Nazis found out about us, the whole town would be in danger, not just us. That's why no one can tell on us! The people of Moissac are wonderful. We're all in on the same secret!" Sarah's face shone with delight at this wonderful conspiracy. All Edith could do was shake her head in amazement.

A group of Jewish girl scouts living in the house in Moissac.

As the girls got ready for bed, Germaine, their counselor, arrived.

"I've come to turn out the lights, girls, and to meet our new family member. Welcome, Edith," she said warmly. "I'm sure you have already learned much of what you need to know from Sarah." Sarah grinned. "I'm the counselor for this room. I'll help get you settled and make sure you have everything you need."

But the only thing that Edith needed was her family, and this young woman, not much older than Therese, wouldn't be able to give her that.

Edith could do no more than nod. She was too exhausted to talk. She crawled under her blanket and reached for her pillow, clinging to one small hope: *Everyone here is just like me. Could they become a family for me too?* It was too soon to know; but somehow, even in the dark in this strange place, Edith felt safe. She hoped and prayed that she would stay that way, and that the running would stop. She thought about Mutti and Papa and hoped that they would also be safe. That was the last thought she had before her eyes closed for the night.

# CHAPTER 7

## The House in Moissac

The wake-up bell rang just as the first of the sun's rays trickled in through the large window. Edith opened her eyes, stretched, and sat up. That was the best sleep she could remember! Her thoughts then drifted to Mutti, but she quickly pulled them back: she had to focus on the present.

Sarah was already making her bed, folding the blanket carefully over the sheets, and fluffing her pillow. "Good morning," she said. "Make your bed, and I'll show you where the bathroom is."

A row of sinks lined one wall of the bathroom. A small towel hung above each basin, with a cubbyhole above it. Edith placed her toothbrush and comb in an empty one. She splashed warm water over her face, scrubbing away the grime with a facecloth and a piece of soap. On either side of her, girls were chatting with one another as they washed. On the way back to their room, Sarah greeted several girls and boys from other rooms and introduced them to Edith.

"Hello, Suzanne," she said. "Good morning, Eric. Hello, Eve. This is Edith Schwalb. She's new."

Even Ida, who had first told Edith about Moissac, was there to greet her. "I'm glad you made it here," Ida said.

All the girls and boys stopped to say hello and welcome Edith. Everyone was friendly. Everyone smiled and greeted her. It was a comforting start to her first day.

Back in their room, the girls dressed quickly and then began their chores. Everyone had something to do: one girl swept the floor with the big broom that was kept behind the door; Sarah grabbed a cloth and dusted the window and bed frames; someone then lined the beds up in an exact formation.

Germaine entered the room and asked, "How did you sleep, Edith?"

Edith shrugged. "Better than I thought I would."

"Good," Germaine replied. "Now, grab a cloth. The quicker we do the chores, the quicker we get breakfast."

Food! Suddenly Edith was starving. Before they left home, her stomach had been in knots and had barely held down a slurp of Mutti's soup. Now its grumbling encouraged her to pick up a soft cloth and help Sarah with the dusting.

Finally, chores were done, and the girls lined up to walk down the stairs and into the dining room.

About a hundred girls and boys, with their counselors, were gathered around their tables when Edith, Sarah, and the others entered. Edith wondered about Gaston. He was staying in a smaller house next door, set up especially for the youngest children. She would go to see him as soon as she could.

"This is the table for our room," said Sarah. "But first, I want you to meet Bouli." She steered Edith toward a tall, thin man standing off to one side, greeting some children.

"Bouli," said Sarah, tugging on his suit jacket. "This is Edith Schwalb."

Bouli Simon eyed Edith closely through his black-rimmed glasses. Instinctively, Edith grabbed her nose. *You won't put any drops in me*, she thought. But Bouli smiled, took Edith's hand in his, and shook it warmly.

"Ah, Edith," he said. "Bienvenue! Welcome. We're so pleased to have you in our house. Sarah here is the perfect guide. She'll tell you all about our routines. But if you need anything else, Shatta and I are here to help."

His fatherly gaze brought a lump to Edith's throat, but she managed a quick thank-you before taking her place at the table next to Sarah. Breakfast was wonderful: oatmeal with cream, thick slices of toast with preserves, and hot coffee with steaming milk and sugar. While the children ate, Bouli patrolled the aisles of the dining room and, just as Sarah had warned, whenever he spotted someone with elbows on the table, he rapped a sharp reminder. The children straightened quickly each time Bouli came close, but they weren't afraid. They smiled at him and continued eating.

After breakfast, Edith joined the other children her age for the walk to the local school. Sarah told her that the older boys and girls studied at the house, either in the classrooms or in the workshops, where they learned photography, bookbinding, and carpentry.

Once outside, Edith could see the whole three-storey, gray-stone building for the first time. The house sat in the middle of the street called Port à Moissac. Its shiny brass number 18 glistened above the door in the early morning sunlight. Edith glanced up at the windows. Each was adorned with a wrought-iron balcony and two full-length wooden shutters with bold crisscross designs. Trees lined the walkway to the house and the street. Across the road was a big bridge over the Tarn River, from which a cool breeze drifted in. Edith took a deep breath and filled her lungs with fresh air. She was so happy to be outside, even if she was going to school.

The children lined up in pairs behind one of the counselors. Sarah grabbed Edith's hand and maneuvered her into place. When an orderly line had been formed, the counselor raised her hand, and the children set off.

Edith groaned as she entered the small schoolhouse. *Another change in the middle of the school year*, she thought, *and more schoolwork I won't understand!* All the moves had made it difficult to keep up with the other students.

"Excuse me, madame," Edith said timidly. "I'm new here."

Madame Beaufort peered at Edith for a long moment, wrinkling her brow and appearing baffled. Then her face softened, and she nodded. "Oh yes! The new girl. And your name?"

"Edith Schwalb. I was told to speak with you."

"Of course. Shatta told me you would be here today. Come. I'll show you where your seat will be, and you can meet some of the other girls. Don't look so frightened, Edith. No one is going to bite you!"

The teacher led her to a desk near the front of the room. "Sit close to me," she said. "That way, I'll be able to give you some extra help if you need it. I understand that you have missed a great deal of school these past few years. But don't worry. You'll catch up."

Edith was amazed. Most teachers had been indifferent to her struggles with schoolwork, but Madame Beaufort was not mean at all. Still, that didn't make the work any easier, which Edith found out as soon as Madame Beaufort handed her the math assignment. The numbers swam in front of her eyes.

"Are you having trouble with that?" A girl peered over her shoulder.

Children from the house in Moissac on their way to school.

"No," Edith said quickly. "I can manage." She slunk low in her chair. It was dangerous to attract attention. Mutti had told her again and again: keep to yourself, be invisible. But this girl would not go away.

"I'll help," the girl insisted. She slid onto Edith's chair, pushing her aside slightly. "I'm Renée," she said. "Here's how to do it." Quickly, she explained the calculations, and coached Edith until she understood. Before long, the assignment was completed.

"Thank you," Edith whispered.

"You're welcome. I love teaching," Renée replied. "You're from the Jewish house, aren't you?"

Edith froze.

"It's okay. We know all about you," Renée continued matter-of-factly. "We're all the same, Catholics and Jews. That's what my mother says, and that's what I think too."

Edith sat in astonishment. Nothing made sense here in Moissac. Teachers were gentle, children were kind, and being Jewish seemed to be okay. Even school might be fun.

As the bell rang to end classes, Edith whispered, "Sophie, I'm doing okay."

# CHAPTER 8

## Be Prepared

After school, the girls returned to the house to complete their school assignments. Edith worked through her homework with a confidence she had not felt in some time. When her last piece of writing was done, she sat back on her bed and smiled proudly. *If only Therese could see me now*, she thought.

"I'm done too," said Sarah, putting her book aside. "I want to take you to choir practice, but first we need to do some chores. 'Work before play,' Shatta always says. Our job is to peel potatoes. And," Sarah whispered, "if we're lucky, Cook will give us a treat. Let's go!"

The cook was a round woman, almost as wide as she was short. When Sarah and Edith entered the kitchen, she was sweating over a big pot on the stove. She had to stand on tiptoe to stir the soup. Her face was red, and her voice made a soft wheezing sound as she quietly chanted a hymn.

"Sarah, ma petite, my sweet one," the cook cried. "You're my favorite young boarder and my best helper."

Sarah grinned and whispered to Edith, "She says that to all of us." Then Sarah turned back to the cook. "This is Edith," Sarah said. "She's new here."

"Aren't you a dear!" the cook exclaimed, wrapping Edith in a hug that nearly smothered her. "Look at those beautiful big eyes — just like my youngest. I've got six at home — every one a gift from the Lord." She crossed herself and muttered a quick blessing.

Edith stifled a giggle. It had been such a long time since anyone had thought her pretty. The jolly woman probably found a compliment for all the children, but that didn't matter — Edith liked her immediately.

"I'd take you all home if I could," the cook continued. "But my poor husband! It's hard enough for him to feed our six. How would he feed a hundred?" The cook's laugh was so jolly that her whole body jiggled, and Edith and Sarah had to laugh with her.

"Take an apron, girls, and a paring knife each," the cook said, wiping the tears from her eyes.

In no time, there was a huge pile of potato peelings in the sink. Working together had made the chore fun. As Edith and Sarah were about to leave, the cook smiled at them. "Did you think I had forgotten?" she asked. "A chocolate truffle for each of you." The girls thanked the cook and ran out of the kitchen to savor their treats.

"Hello, Sarah," someone called. Sarah and Edith turned to face an older boy.

"Hi, Eric. Edith, you remember Eric. You met him yesterday."

Edith smiled. She had met so many new people that she could barely tell one from the other. Vaguely she recalled meeting this young boy in the hallway on the day she had arrived. Eric was about sixteen, serious-looking, with wild unruly hair and the darkest eyes Edith had ever seen. He stared at her intently until she had to look away.

"Eric knows more than anyone I've ever met. And he can do almost everything, too." Sarah giggled. "He's a photographer, a bookbinder, and works in the woodworking shop." Sarah ticked off Eric's accomplishments on her fingers, one by one.

Eric shrugged. "A bit of this and a bit of that. It all comes in handy."

"Do you need some help?" asked Sarah.

Eric was loaded down with a large tent folded up and slung across his back. Several cooking pots dangled from his belt. Sarah and Edith grabbed the pots, and all three brought the equipment into the dining room, where children were rolling sleeping bags and folding tents. Shatta, at the far end of the dining hall, looked up briefly and waved, before shouting, "Group leaders, check all the tents very carefully! Make sure there are no holes. Have your teams pile them up over here once you've inspected them."

"Are kids going camping?" asked Edith.

Eric Goldfarb

Eric chuckled. "We're ready to go at a moment's notice. That's one of our mottoes here."

Edith was puzzled. "Go where? And why quickly?"

"You're new," Eric replied, "so you haven't been part of a raid. But you will, and then you'll understand." He unfolded his tent and bent to inspect it.

Sarah looked at Edith reassuringly. "We really are safe here. But the Nazis come through now and then, looking for Jews."

A roundup! Fear gripped Edith's throat. "My papa was taken in a round up," she croaked.

"That's why we're prepared," replied Eric. "Look around you — we've got tents, sleeping bags, lanterns, pots, pans, rope, knives, compasses, gaiters, backpacks, maps, and food, all ready to go." Eric rattled off the camping gear, checking the equipment against a mental list. "Before a raid comes, we're out of here."

"But how do you know when there'll be a raid?" Edith was beginning to panic. "And where does everyone go?"

"We're warned if the Nazis are coming," said Sarah calmly. "The mayor of Moissac gets word to Shatta, and all of us leave for a few days to go camping in the hills. When it's safe, we come back."

What was it that Shatta had said, Edith struggled to recall. Shatta had talked about the mayor of Moissac when Edith first arrived at the house. She said that the mayor was a friend and would help protect the Jewish children. Is this what Shatta had meant?

"Don't worry. It will all make sense," said Eric easily, before moving off to help some of the other children. "You'll see soon enough."

Sarah gently steered Edith from the dining room. Edith felt numb. How could she not worry? She didn't want to have to find out what happened in a raid. She didn't want to have to run again. Suddenly she didn't want to be here at all.

The choir in Moissac — Henri Milstein, the choir director, is in the middle. Edith is in the second row from the bottom, just to the right of Henri's arm.

When Sarah finally introduced Edith to Henri, the choir director, Edith stood mutely and hung her head. Sarah whispered something to Henri, who nodded. "Why don't you just sit and listen to us today, Edith. You'll join in the next time."

Edith slumped onto a chair. Henri took his place in front of the girls and boys and raised a small baton. The sound of blended voices filled the room. Edith wanted to listen, to lose herself in the simple beauty of the harmony; but she was too agitated. Just this morning, she had woken up feeling safe. The cook had made her feel loved and secure. Now she felt as if she had been dropped out a window and was about to hit the ground.

There were more than one hundred children in the house in Moissac. How would everyone get out in time? When the Nazis came for Papa in the middle of the night, there was no time to escape. No one knew the raid was coming. Even if the mayor warned them here in Moissac, would they be trapped with no time to run?

There was no such thing in the world as a safe place, only places to avoid danger a little while longer. Moissac was a trick. Mutti had been wrong to bring her here. Edith closed her eyes and took a deep breath. She already felt trapped. And there was nowhere for her to go. She could only wait and see what would happen.

# CHAPTER 9

## Gaston

It was several days before Edith was finally able to visit Gaston in the smaller house next door. She had wanted to visit sooner; but her days were too busy and there was no spare time. Perhaps Shatta had orchestrated it that way, wanting the children in each room to bond with one another.

Edith opened the heavy wooden door of the house and climbed the stairs to Gaston's room on the second floor. She walked in quietly, to find her little brother lying on his bed, staring at the ceiling.

"Gaston," Edith whispered.

He turned his head slightly, then leapt up and wrapped his arms around her.

"Edith!" he cried, clinging with all his might, almost afraid that if he let go, she would disappear. "Where have you been?"

Edith hugged Gaston back tightly. She promised herself that from now on, she would make sure to visit him more often.

"I'm here now, Gaston. Come, tell me how you are." She gently pulled his arms away from her neck and steered him back onto his bed. She jumped up next to him and stared into his round eyes. Gaston had always been so special — spoiled and doted on. From the day he was born, Edith was happy to have a little brother — someone else to play with and even boss around at times. But she had to admit that she was also a little jealous. After all, *she* had been her Papa's little girl and the baby of the family. Now she was replaced with this beautiful blond boy. And he commanded everyone's attention. Gaston was always busy. He was energetic and full of life. Mutti had to watch him every second or he might jump off a table, wander away, or get into some kind of trouble. It was hard to imagine that that same lively child was this sad little boy who sat in front of Edith now.

Gaston stared at his sister. It was as if someone had turned the light out in his once bright eyes. Edith reached out to brush a curl off of his forehead. "Are you all right?" she asked. Gaston hesitated, and then nodded slightly. "Is there anything you want?" she tried again.

He looked deeply into her eyes. "I want Mutti." The room filled with the sound of his painful sobbing.

Memories of Mutti had been drifting in and out of Edith's mind like the soft waves she saw on the river from her dormitory window. Where *was* Mutti, Edith wondered. Was she safe? Did she have enough to eat? A bed to sleep in? Was she afraid?

Edith sighed and reached out to hug Gaston. "I miss her too, Gaston — and Papa and Therese," she said.

The two children talked softly as the day was ending, but soon it was time for Edith to leave.

"When will you come back, Edith?"

"Tomorrow," she promised. "I'll come back tomorrow."

"You won't," Gaston cried angrily. "You're just like Mutti and Papa. You're going to leave and you won't come back."

"Gaston, listen to me, I'm not leaving you. Look out your window and you can see my room. I'll be back tomorrow." With that, Edith turned and left his room.

*Poor Gaston*, thought Edith. His whole life had been filled with uncertainty and change. Gaston did not know what it was like to play in a playground, to slurp ice cream in a café, or to watch Papa playing soccer while the crowd cheered. But maybe it was better not to know what you were missing.

When Edith walked out of Gaston's house, it was overcast and rainy, as if the sky was weeping for her. Here in Moissac were kind people who looked after her and fed her and made sure her clothes were clean and her homework was done. Shatta and Bouli treated all the children as if they were their own. But Edith still felt lonely. Shatta and Bouli were not her parents. The other children were not her brothers and sisters. They were family only because of their common despair.

◦◦◦

As Edith approached her house, the sound of singing interrupted her sad thoughts. "What's going on?" she asked, as Germaine rushed by carrying pots and candlesticks.

"It's Shabbat," her counselor replied. "The sun is about to set, and we're preparing the house for the Sabbath."

Edith found Sarah brushing her long, beautiful hair in the dormitory. "Friday night is wonderful here," Sarah said. "We try to dress up. The cook makes special food, and a rabbi even comes to lead the service. We sing songs, and it's all so beautiful."

Edith shook her head in disbelief. In Vienna, her family had celebrated the Sabbath. She had attended synagogue with her father and had loved to listen to the hymns and prayers. But then the family had stopped practicing their religion in order not to draw attention. Now it seemed the children in Moissac could be Jewish and not afraid. It was so confusing! One minute she was fearful and despairing; the next she felt snug in a protective cocoon.

"Come," cried Sarah, as she tied her hair back with a bright red ribbon. "We'll pick some flowers for the tables."

The field behind the house was full of early spring flowers. The fragrance of wild anemones — purple, red, and blue — filled the early evening air. Edith inhaled deeply. Anemones were Mutti's favorite flowers; finding them was like finding a piece of Mutti herself.

Edith and Sarah brought armfuls of flowers into the dining room, where girls were polishing candlesticks and laying down white tablecloths and special dishes. They finished arranging flowers in pots and vases on every table just as the rest of the children entered to take their seats.

"Shabbat Shalom," whispered Sarah. "I wish you peace on this Sabbath."

"Shabbat Shalom," replied Edith. "Peace for us all."

# CHAPTER 10

## Help Your Neighbor

As she had promised, Edith visited Gaston every day, always wearing her bravest face. She never said a word about the raids or the camping trips. She smiled and made him believe that everything would be fine.

"Papa will come home soon, Gaston," Edith said one day, as they sat together on the front stoop of Gaston's house. "And when he does, Mutti will bring us home, too. And aren't we well taken care of? Mutti was very clever sending us here."

Slowly but surely the fantasy rubbed off on Edith. She realized that if you pretended that things were okay, eventually you began to believe it. Besides, nothing terrible *was* happening. People didn't call her bad names; in fact, the townspeople were friendly. There were no arrests of Jews in Moissac, no beatings on the street. Even when Shatta and Bouli talked about the war — Jews being arrested in Romania, Yugoslavia, and Greece; more and more concentration camps being built — the events felt far away. Of course there were still difficult times, especially in the quiet of night when the sadness of being without her parents would creep into Edith's dreams. But she would force herself to shake off the thoughts and carry on.

That became easier because there was so much to do: chores, school and homework, and choir, which Edith now enjoyed. But camping skills — the knowledge that could save their lives — always came first. After all, the house in Moissac was established on the philosophy of the Scouting movement. "Be prepared," Shatta had told Edith the day she arrived. The young residents learned how to build a fire and tie knots, to follow a trail and tell time by the sun. And every day the children exercised to build their muscles and endurance.

"Scouts must be strong, alert, and knowledgeable," Bouli explained one day, as he led Edith and the others on a hike. "Stay together," he commanded as he walked quickly up a steep hill. "Push those legs. Breathe that fresh air." Edith struggled to keep up, overwhelmed by memories of her escape from Vienna through the forests. Her legs throbbed, just as they had during that long flight. And this time, Papa was not there to carry her.

Yet, with each passing day, Edith's body felt stronger and her pain lessened. She was developing her leg muscles, and a healthy glow had appeared on her cheeks.

One warm spring afternoon, during a short break in their hike, Bouli invited the children to gather around him. The sun was still high in the sky, its bright rays beating down on the heads of the young hikers. Edith sat down, picked up a small flower, and absently pulled off the petals.

*One is for Mutti,*
*Two is for me,*
*Three is for Papa*
*and my family.*

"What are you thinking about?" asked Sarah. "You look a million miles away."

Edith felt far away. She hadn't thought of this silly poem since family picnics in the countryside around Vienna; and now the association triggered an intense longing for her family. She never knew what would set off these yearnings, and they cropped up quite unexpectedly — while eating breakfast, or walking to school or even dusting her room. Edith shook her head, trying to shake the aching away. "It's okay, Sarah. I'm back now."

Bouli called for everyone's attention and then began to talk. "Children, what is the purpose of Scouting?"

"To learn new skills."

"To do your best at all times."

"To be strong."

Bouli nodded. "Those are all important ideas. What else?"

"To help people," Eric called out.

"Exactly!" said Bouli. *"Service to others* — that is the true purpose of the Scouting movement. Helping the people around you. Now, where do we see examples of this in our lives?"

"You and Shatta are helping all of us by keeping us here," said Sarah.

"The people in town help us," another child responded, "by keeping the secret that we are Jews."

"Very good!" said Bouli. "The people of Moissac, by staying silent, by keeping the secret of our Judaism, protect us. Even though it is dangerous. Even though they must risk their lives to keep us safe. They are the perfect example of service and the courage to do what is right, even in the face of danger."

Doing what was right. Edith let this message sink in. That's why the people of Moissac were helping the Jewish children. Not because they were being paid, like the farmer who had taken Mutti's pearl necklace, or like the Belgian prison guards whom Mutti had bribed to release Papa; but simply because it was right.

"Come here," Sarah called, breaking into Edith's thoughts. "I'm going to teach you a double half-hitch. It's the knot that's used to tie down a tent." Edith took a deep breath, moved over to sit next to Sarah, and stared down at a pile of ropes. "Pretend this branch is a tent stake," said Sarah. "Hold the end of the rope in your right hand. Now loop it around the branch twice, cross it over to make an X. Then push the end of the rope through that hole at the end of the X, and pull tight." Edith followed Sarah's movements closely.

"That's it!" exclaimed Sarah. "You're a natural."

Edith practiced again and again. By the end of the afternoon, she could quickly and efficiently lash pieces of wood together and join ropes of different thickness. She had also learned how to roll a sleeping bag into a compact bundle. To her amazement, Edith was good at these skills, and enjoyed learning. Every now and then, her mind wandered to thoughts of roundups and raids by the Nazi soldiers. She could not quite believe she would ever really need to put these new skills to use. But she didn't want to think about that.

By the time the camping session ended, Edith was tired but satisfied. She followed Bouli down the hill and back into the house. She flopped down on her bed, thinking she had only a few minutes to clean up before supper.

Just then, Eve entered the room, silently pulled her suitcase from under her bed, and began packing.

"Going on vacation?" asked Sarah playfully. "That's why you weren't on the hike?"

Eve looked up. "I'm leaving." Her voice was low and somber. The smile instantly left Sarah's face.

"Leaving?" asked Sarah. "Where are you going?"

"My parents have come to get me. They've decided I'll be safer with them. We're going to Switzerland. We've got relatives there. We're going to go across France and over the mountains."

Leaving? No one had ever left the house. Edith had never thought it possible. All her pleasure in the hike disappeared. If only Mutti would come for her! That would be the greatest gift of all — to be reunited with her parents.

No one spoke, but all the girls gazed enviously at Eve.

Eve closed her suitcase. "I'll miss all of you," she said, hugging the girls one by one.

Edith followed her downstairs, where Shatta stood with a man and woman. The man took the small suitcase from Eve and shook hands with Shatta.

"Merci, Madame Simon. Thank you for taking care of our daughter."

"Please, monsieur," begged Shatta. "Don't take the child. This is the safest place for her."

"She's safest with us," the woman replied. "What could be safer than being with your family?"

Edith crouched on the stairs as Shatta's voice became more urgent. "We all know that France has become as dangerous as the rest of Europe for Jews. We are protected here by the people of this town. This is not the case outside of Moissac."

Eve's father shook his head, and the three left the house. Shatta walked toward her office, hunched and exhausted. It unnerved Edith to see Shatta — always so strong and confident in front of the children — look defeated.

Edith needed to talk to someone, but she was not sure that Sarah would be able to make sense of this. Noise from the bookbindery shop at the back of the main floor gave Edith an idea. Eric would be the perfect person to talk to. He was smart and realistic.

"Hello." Eric smiled as Edith approached.

"Hi, Eric." Edith looked down at the pile of papers, scissors, and thick thread in front of him. "What's all this?"

"You see that man over there?" Eric pointed toward an older man at the other end of the room, surrounded by young people.

"He's one of the best bookbinders in France, and he comes to teach us. I've been training with him for a few months now, and I'm getting pretty good."

"Show me," Edith said. It would be a good distraction from her confusion about Eve.

"First, you have to fold a large sheet to look like this." Eric picked up a pile of papers from his workbench. "Then, the sections are sewn into the cover, one at a time. You sew the whole book with a single thread, so you have to make sure it's long enough." He wove a thick needle in and out of a pile of pages, pulling tightly with each even stitch. "If we're lucky we get leather for the covers, but this thick cardboard works pretty well. Here's the first book I made here."

Eric reached under the table and proudly pulled out a small rectangular album. It had a deep brown cover with black paper pages. Edith bent to look at the perfectly spaced stitches that he had sewn. The book was filled with photographs, many of Moissac and its children. "I took the pictures and developed them myself," added Eric proudly.

Edith flipped through the pages. "Who's this?" she asked, pointing to a photo of a young couple with three small children.

"My parents. My brother and sister. And that's me," he said, indicating the youngest child. The picture was taken in Poland. That's where I was born. But I grew up in Germany. We escaped in 1939."

"Do you know where they are now?"

Eric shrugged. "All over. My sister was sent to England, my brother to China. My parents managed to send a couple of letters through the Red Cross, but they were only allowed twenty-five words, so I didn't learn very much."

Edith stared at the picture. "Eric, if your parents arrived here and wanted to take you away with them, would you go?"

He frowned. "I've been away from my family for so long that I can't really picture us together. Besides, I'm old enough to look after myself."

"But if they did come," insisted Edith, "would you leave Moissac? Eve's parents came for her today. They say that Eve is safe with them. Shatta says she's safer here. What do you think?"

Eric paused thoughtfully. "I trust Shatta," he said at last. "This house has been here for four years, and so far everyone has stayed safe. You can't say the same for the Jews elsewhere." With that, he turned back to his work.

A few days later, after supper, Edith was helping to tidy the dining room. After the other girls had left, she hesitantly approached Shatta. "Have you heard from Eve?" Edith asked. By now, everyone knew that Eve had left with her parents.

Shatta shook her head. "The news is not good," she said, her voice catching. "Our sources tell me that Eve and her family have been arrested and sent to a concentration camp. All we can do now is pray that they survive."

# CHAPTER 11

## July 8, 1943
## A Special Day

Edith thought about Eve for weeks after that, playing the scene of Eve's departure over in her mind like a record. After that night in the dining room, Shatta had refused to say much more about Eve, and Edith understood how painful her leaving was for Shatta. Each child in the house was like one of her own. To lose one was like losing a member of her family. Shatta could be tough on the outside, but she was vulnerable when it came to her children. As for Edith, seeing Eve's parents had just intensified her longing for her own family. Being with them had always felt safe; yet, that was when Papa had been taken away. No one had been arrested here in Moissac, at least not yet. Edith felt more confused than ever.

One morning, several weeks later, Edith woke up before the bell, rolled over, and stretched. The sound of birds singing drifted through the open windows, and she lay still, listening. Wait — it was too quiet. She sat up and looked around the room. The dormitory was empty.

Edith was suddenly wide-awake. *Where is everyone? They've gone*, she thought, panic rising. *They've gone and left me behind. The*

*Nazis are coming and someone forgot to wake me in time to leave. I'm the only one they'll find!*

She shook her head and scolded herself. "Stop making things worse! Calm down, Edith." The sound of her voice echoed in the empty room. Just then, Sarah and all Edith's roommates burst through the door.

"Happy birthday, Edith!" The girls crowded around, cheering and applauding. "You took forever to wake up!"

She was so startled that she couldn't speak. It was July 8, 1943. She was eleven years old. How could she have forgotten?

"Come on, sleepyhead," said Sarah. "Get dressed and let's go to breakfast. There's a surprise for you."

Edith smiled gratefully. Sarah had remembered her special day! The girls washed, dressed, and finished their chores in record time. Edith flew down the stairs behind Sarah, burst into the dining room — and stopped in her tracks. Everyone in the house was there, standing, waiting for her. Henri picked up his baton and the choir began to sing. "Bonne fête à toi. Happy birthday to you." Soon everyone had joined in. Shatta and Bouli gave Edith a warm hug and wished her a happy birthday. She was overwhelmed. There was birthday cake and flowers on her table, and at her place, a small package.

"It's not much," Sarah said apologetically, "but at least we remembered."

Eyes shining brightly, Edith opened the package and found a red zippered case. She turned it over in her hands.

"Open it," cried Sarah.

Edith unzipped the leather case. It was a manicure set, complete with a small pair of scissors, a clipper, and a nail file. She gave Sarah a huge hug. "Thank you so much," she whispered. "It's the best present I ever received." And it was. Yet compared with her parties and presents in Vienna, it was so small.

Edith had a fleeting memory of past birthdays. Mutti baked beautiful birthday cakes, and Therese was especially kind. Papa took her shopping for a new dress, and her friends and cousins showered her with presents. In Belgium and France, she had celebrated her birthday quietly, just with parents and siblings. But now she didn't even know where her parents were. Edith shook these thoughts away. It was her birthday, and for this moment, on this day, she was determined to be happy.

༒

There was one more birthday surprise to come. It was the least expected, but the best present she could have ever imagined receiving. As Edith arrived back from school that day, Shatta called to her.

"First of all, happy birthday again, my dear," Shatta said warmly. "Has it been a good day for you?"

"Oh yes, Shatta," Edith replied. "The best day in a long time."

"Well, I think it's going to get even better," Shatta said mysteriously. "There is a surprise for you in my office." Edith looked puzzled and a little wary. Shatta laughed and gently pushed Edith toward her open office door.

A woman stood in front of her. "Mutti!" Edith shouted, and flew into her mother's arms.

"Oh my darling, it's so good to hold you," Mutti whispered, as they stood wrapped in a loving embrace. Finally, Mutti took Edith by the shoulders and held her at arm's length. "Let me look at you, birthday girl. Ah, only four months and you look so much older. You're so grown up!"

Edith's face glowed as she gazed into her mother's eyes. *This must be a dream*, she thought. She closed her eyes tightly for a moment, but when she opened them again, her mother was still in front of her.

Edith suddenly frowned. "But you, Mutti, you're so thin." It was true. Mutti looked haggard and sickly. Her eyes were sunken, and her once beautiful skin lay in soft wrinkled folds.

Mutti shook her head. "It's hard to get food. Everything is rationed, and I don't have a ration book. But don't worry," she said, seeing the pain in Edith's look. "I'm fine, and lucky to be with a good family. Thank goodness you are here. You and Gaston — both safe. I've just seen him and he looks wonderful."

Edith felt a sudden sharp pang of guilt: she was well fed and taken care of, while Mutti …

Mutti raised Edith's face with her hand. "Knowing that my children are safe gives me strength and nourishment." Mutti sighed. "Come, my darling. Sit with me and tell me everything."

And Edith did. She talked about the routine of the house, and about how kind Shatta and Bouli were. She told Mutti about Sarah, Eric, and the other children. She talked about school and how well she seemed to be doing. Mutti listened hungrily to every word and, as Edith told her stories, seemed to gather strength from them.

Then, it was Mutti's turn. Her story was harder to listen to. She was hiding with a farming family north of Moissac; Therese was with another family close by. Both were working as maids, cleaning and cooking. Mutti saw Therese occasionally, but they had to be careful not to be seen together, in case someone became suspicious. And while the families hiding them were caring and generous, Mutti added, "There are plenty of people only too happy to turn in a couple of Jewish women." Still, they were both out of harm's way, she assured Edith.

"And Papa?" Edith asked.

Mutti shook her head. "No, no word."

That was painful to hear. The silence that followed hurt so much that Edith quickly changed the subject. "How did you get here, Mutti? It's so far, all alone."

"I didn't want to use the trains. I was too afraid someone might ask for identity papers. So I rode in trucks and hay wagons — farmers are often willing to help a woman traveling alone, without asking questions. It took two days, but it's been worth every second," she added, hugging Edith once more.

Edith didn't want to let go — didn't want to think that her mother might walk out the door again. But all too soon, it was time for Mutti to leave.

"Please don't go, Mutti!" Edith begged hoarsely. She desperately clung to her mother. This parting was even harder than the first one, four months earlier. "When will you come back? When will I see you again?"

Mutti pulled away gently. "I will try to visit again, but I can't promise. You are always in my heart," she whispered, then turned and walked out the door.

Edith sat alone, aching with sadness. Finally, she walked slowly upstairs and slumped on her bed. She told Sarah about Mutti's visit and how hard the goodbye had been. But Sarah's reaction was a shock.

"Stop whining," she said. "You're lucky you have a mother who can visit. Look around, Edith. Most of us don't know where our mothers are. We don't even know if they're alive." With that, Sarah turned her back on Edith and started her homework.

Edith felt as if her friend had slapped her. She glanced uneasily around the room. Some girls were glaring at her with the same hostility she had seen when Eve's parents came for her. Others looked envious, and turned away with tears in their eyes. "I'm sorry, everyone," Edith said in a small voice. She knew she was luckier than the other girls, but that didn't make her feel any less miserable or less abandoned.

"It's my birthday today, Sophie," Edith whispered into her pillow. "Happy birthday to me. I got my mother as a present — but then she was taken away." Her tears fell quietly onto her pillow.

# CHAPTER 12
## The Nazis Are Coming

Edith awoke early the next morning. She had slept little. Her eyes were puffy from crying, and her head felt as heavy as her heart. Her birthday had been such a jumble of emotions: the excitement of having the whole house remember her special day, the thrill of seeing Mutti, and her despair when Mutti left. Edith didn't want to talk to the other girls this morning; those feeling were confusing, too. So she dressed quietly, made her bed, and wandered down the hall. The cook would be up and in the kitchen. Maybe Edith could help her. Just listening to Cook's stories would be a welcome distraction.

Edith made her way downstairs, savoring the peacefulness. Soon the house would be buzzing with activity. As she crossed the front hallway, she was startled by a heavy knock at the main door. No one else was about, so she pulled the big wooden door open.

A man Edith vaguely recognized from town stood, hat in hand, and bowed slightly when she greeted him.

"Is Madame Simon here?" he asked. He shifted from one foot to the other and glanced over his shoulder, nervously checking up and down the street. "It's important," he added, as Edith stepped aside to allow him to enter.

"This way, monsieur." Edith motioned the man to follow her across the hall to Shatta's office and knocked softly on the door.

"Entrez! Come in," called Shatta.

Edith peered into the office. "There's someone to see you, Shatta — a man from town."

Shatta quickly strode to the door, shook his hand, and led him inside. Then she turned to Edith. "Join your friends, my dear. Thank you." The door closed in Edith's face.

Something was not right — and that made Edith uneasy. There were often visitors to the house: the man who brought eggs, the women who cleaned, the doctor who visited the sick. But this seemed different. Perhaps it was the man's nervous manner. Maybe it was Shatta closing the door on her. Whatever it was, Edith put her ear to the door to listen. The voices inside the office were soft but urgent, and she strained to catch what was being said.

"The mayor has just received word that there will be a raid on Moissac — tomorrow, perhaps even later today," the man was saying. "He urges you to gather the children and leave quickly."

Shatta was saying something in reply, but Edith had heard enough. She stumbled blindly through the hall. Her head was spinning, her heart pounding. She had been waiting for this nightmare, had fantasized that it would happen. But this was not a dream. The emergency was real.

Somehow, Edith managed to make it up the stairs and back into her room. Sarah and the other girls were up and dressing.

"What's wrong?" Sarah asked, as Edith stormed into the dormitory.

Edith pulled Sarah over to a corner. "Shatta is talking to this man," she blurted out, struggling to calm herself. "He says the Nazis are about to raid Moissac. He said we have to leave. Sarah, what's going to happen to us?" All of the uncertainty that Edith had felt toward Sarah the night before vanished. Edith needed Sarah now; she needed an ally to help her understand what was happening.

Sarah nodded calmly. "We'll be fine, Edith."

Before she had a chance to say more, Germaine rushed in, ordering everyone downstairs for a meeting. Shatta and Bouli were waiting.

"Children, we must go camping. I've just received word from our friend the mayor." Shatta's voice was controlled but firm. "The soldiers are coming to Moissac to look for Jews. Our gear is all ready. So quickly, run to your rooms and grab any last things you might need."

Like well-rehearsed actors, the children went into action in an orderly but urgent manner. Edith pushed her way through the crowd and stopped in front of Shatta, who was still instructing her staff in preparation for their departure.

"Don't make the beds," she commanded. "There's no time. Be sure every group has its food packs. Bouli, bring the medical supplies." Shatta kept shouting instructions over the rising noise.

"Shatta," Edith asked, breathless and frightened. "What about my brother and the little ones? Where are they going? What's going to happen to them?"

Shatta placed her arm around Edith's shoulders. "Gaston and the younger children are too small to hike into the woods," she said. "They are being hidden in homes around Moissac. We have many friends here in town, Edith, enough to ensure all of them will be safe."

In that instant, the house was ready for their "camping trip." The children were fit and had the skills they would need. Regular staff meetings had been held to perfect the plans. Cases and sleeping bags were ready to go. Food was packed. Camping kits were organized. The tents, which weeks earlier had been inspected, were folded and packed. The house was set for flight.

"Come on. Let's get our things. Don't be afraid." Sarah squeezed Edith's hand tightly. "I've done this before. We'll be safe. You'll see."

How many times in the past four years had she been told that she would be safe? Papa, Mutti, Shatta, and now Sarah had given her the same assurance. Would she really be safe today? The memory of fleeing Vienna and then Brussels came back to Edith in a powerful vision as she grabbed some clothing and ran out of her room.

On the way down the stairs, Edith passed Eric, who was struggling up against the current of children. "Did you forget something, Eric?" Edith asked.

Eric Goldfarb

"I'm not going," he said. "The older boys are staying here."

Edith could not believe what she was hearing. "You're doing *what*? What are you talking about? You'll be arrested."

"Never!" Eric replied. "There are lots of good hiding places in this house — in the attic, behind the woodshed. It's really us older boys the Nazis want. The soldiers may not care about a group of youngsters camping in the woods. But if we're with you, it would make things more dangerous."

Edith grabbed him by the arm. "Stay safe, Eric."

"I'll be here when you get back," he said, smiling. "Don't worry about me."

Edith joined the crowd of children assembled in the dining room. Counselors were calling out the names of children, giving each one a pack with sleeping bags, food, tents, or other gear. When everyone was accounted for, the doors were opened and the children spilled out into the street.

The morning air was warm and the sun shone brightly, as the children and staff marched quickly through the quiet streets, heading for the hills behind Moissac. Shopkeepers were just opening their stores, unlocking their doors, opening blinds and colorful awnings. They nodded slightly as the children walked by but said nothing. *Are they really our friends?* Edith wondered. *When the Nazis come, will they keep our secret?* This would be the true test of their commitment

A photograph of the courtyard of the house in Moissac, taken by Eric Goldfarb.

to the safety of the children. She felt a trickle of sweat work its way down her neck. The pack was heavy, but she could not slow down. She shifted it slightly and picked up her pace.

As she rounded a corner on the outskirts of the town, she glanced up at a small house close to the street. One shutter was open slightly and, behind it, Edith could make out the face of a little girl. As the campers passed by, the child raised her hand and waved. It was the last thing Edith saw before she and the others were led away from Moissac.

# CHAPTER 13

## Camp Volant

S hatta called it Camp Volant — flying camp. It meant that the children would move to a different location every night, in deep thick woods offering shelter and cover.

Shatta and the house leaders led the children farther and farther from the danger in Moissac. The group marched in pairs toward their destination. At first, they passed small farmhouses dotting the countryside around Moissac. In the distance, Edith could make out the farmers tilling their fields. The group leaders marched the children in wide arcs away from these farms. They did not want to be seen, and these farmers could be witnesses to their escape. But eventually the farms disappeared. Then there were only trees, birds, and flowers growing wildly on the hillside to watch the children as they continued their march.

The children spoke little. They needed every ounce of strength to hike and carry their packs. Edith's seemed heavier by the minute. The daily exercise at Moissac had helped strengthen her young legs, but such a long trek was wearing her out. The sun beat down on her

A camping expedition from the house in Moissac.

head, and her legs felt like lead weights. But apart from infrequent, brief stops to drink some water and grab a quick snack, the group leaders urged the children on. Just when Edith felt she could not take one more step, Shatta raised her hand, signaling the group to stop.

Edith dropped her pack and sank down into the tall grass, sweat pouring off her. Sarah flopped next to her. "I don't think I could have gone on for a minute more," said Sarah. Edith nodded. But there was still work to be done.

"We have to set up camp before the sun goes down," Bouli said. "There will be plenty of time to rest after that."

Edith groaned slightly but pulled herself back up. Quickly and efficiently, the group leaders assigned tasks to the children. Some were sent to scrounge for kindling; others gathered larger branches for a fire. Edith and Sarah joined a group of children assembling tents. They unfolded each tent and lined up the ropes and stakes that would secure it to the ground.

Edith hammered a stake into the ground and wound the thick rope around it, using the double half-hitch she had learned at

Moissac. "Loop, pull, and cross over. Loop, pull, and cross over," she whispered, as she secured each rope to a stake.

In a short time, the tents were erected and a fire crackled, big enough to cook the food but not large enough to be seen from a distance. The smell of burning wood mixed with the aroma of a simmering stew soon wafted across the camp. Now everyone could relax.

Edith lay on the cool forest floor. It was so peaceful here in the woods, away from Moissac, away from any danger. Birds sang or squawked at their uninvited visitors, crickets chirped, and small animals scurried in the undergrowth. The fire crackled and the soft sound of voices drifted above Edith's head.

Sarah leaned back against a log. "I'm so hungry, I could eat a tree."

Edith was famished as well, but she had other thoughts on her mind. "Sarah, what if the Nazis find us?"

"They won't," Sarah replied. "No one can find us out here."

"But what if they do?"

"Stop worrying, Edith. We're safe here. Shatta and Bouli have done this many times. They know what they're doing. Besides, what good does it do to worry? There's nothing more we can do. So relax and enjoy the adventure." Sarah turned and looked at her friend. "Just try, Edith. Try to believe we'll be okay."

Edith closed her eyes. She wanted desperately to believe, not only that she and the campers but that Mutti and Papa, Therese and Gaston would be safe. Once she had innocently believed in the future, but now all her hope had evaporated. Besides, this war seemed to be getting worse, and for Jews the news was increasingly bad. Just last week, Bouli had told the children that the Nazis had ordered all Polish Jews be sent to concentration camps. In cities across Europe, the Nazis had moved Jewish citizens into areas enclosed by walls and barbed wire. In these ghettos, Jews were forced to live several families to a small apartment. There were few jobs, little food, sickness, and dirt. And now, the Jews were being sent to the concentration camps, where conditions would be even worse. Yet even as Bouli had told the children this, he reassured them that they were safe.

Edith didn't know what to believe. If such things were happening to Jews elsewhere, how long would it be before they happened here, to her and her friends? Edith couldn't let her guard down — couldn't feel safe the way Sarah seemed to. Every time she felt herself starting to relax, something happened to jolt her back to this scary reality.

As darkness fell, brilliant stars filled the night sky. Edith shivered and reached for a blanket to wrap around her shoulders as the fire burned down. Several children began to sing quietly, their voices blending in a soothing harmony.

"Look," said Sarah, pointing up. "A shooting star. Make a wish, Edith!"

Edith lifted her head in time to see the star carve a path of light across the sky. She fixed her eyes on it and made a wish with all her might.

# CHAPTER 14
## The Scouts of Moissac

The camping trip lasted five days. Each morning the children awoke early, washed, ate breakfast, and then broke camp. Shatta sent a patrol out every morning — five or six hikers accompanied by a counselor. Their job was to search for a place for the next campsite and to make sure that no one was following the larger group. When the coast was clear, all the children set out, carrying their backpacks and gear, marching in pairs.

The fresh forest air was energizing. Edith's pale skin, washed out from months of being too much indoors, became rosy and healthy. Her young body became stronger. The pack, which had felt like a great weight on the first day, became less of a burden, and the daily march became almost effortless. There truly was a sense of freedom in the woods, and Edith became caught up in the adventure.

"We are young Scouts," Shatta said. "This is our opportunity to build character and learn new skills. A Scout is a friend to all — loyal, strong, and capable. Use this time to observe your surroundings. Learn about the forest and the streams. Help one another, and you will be helping yourself."

During those five days, Edith used all the skills she had learned at Moissac and learned many new things. She became more competent at tying complicated knots. She could split wood into kindling. She learned the names of dozens of trees and flowers. She knew which mushrooms and berries were poisonous and which ones could be eaten.

One afternoon, Sarah persuaded Edith to try fishing.

"First, you tie this string to a stick. Careful of the hook," said Sarah. "Now bait the line with this." She held out a squirmy and muddy worm.

"No! I can't do that."

"Of course you can. Take it!"

Edith grimaced and reached for the worm. Holding her breath, she threaded the wriggling creature onto the hook and threw her line into the water. She could make out the silvery silhouettes of fish darting just below the surface.

Suddenly her fishing line stretched tight against the wooden stick. Edith's heart raced as she pulled back on the stick. It bent so far that it threatened to break.

"Don't pull too hard!" yelled Sarah. "It'll get away."

Edith loosened her grip slightly before yanking on the stick again. Back and forth, she fought with the fish, letting it swim out and then tugging it toward shore. A group of friends and counselors cheered her on. Several minutes later, Edith held up the fish triumphantly for everyone to see. That night, there was grilled fish for dinner, and her catch was part of the meal.

On the fifth day, Shatta received word that the Nazis had left the town. The group packed their gear for the last time and headed back to Moissac. Edith was sad to see the camping trip end. It had been an adventure that she would always remember. Sarah had been right — they had remained safe and had had fun. In the forest, Edith had actually forgotten that soldiers were nearby, looking for Jews. She had forgotten that there was any danger.

As soon as the children arrived back at the house, Edith went looking for Gaston. She found him in his room unpacking a few of his belongings.

"Oh, Gaston, I was so worried about you!" Edith squeezed her brother tightly. "Shatta said you were hiding with a family. Were they kind to you?"

Gaston nodded. "I had to pretend I was their son, in case soldiers came. They never did, but I still had to pretend. I had to call the people Maman and Papa. That was hard, but if I closed my eyes and pretended Mutti was there, then I could do it."

"You're very brave, Gaston. Mutti would be proud of you — Papa too."

On the way back to her house, Edith found Eric in the woodworking shop.

"I told you we'd be fine," he said.

"What happened?" Edith asked. "Did the soldiers come?"

"Yes," he said. "Not long after you left. There had to have been ten or twenty of them on patrol. They pounded on the doors.

The cook answered and said that everyone was gone. Of course, she didn't say anything about the fact that we are all Jews here. She just said it was a boarding home for children, and everyone was away for a few days. The soldiers came in, anyway. By then, we were hidden away. Three in the attic behind a trap door, and the rest here behind that stack of wood." Eric pointed to a large wall of lumber piled from floor to ceiling. Sure enough, there was a small cubbyhole behind it, under a hidden staircase, just large enough to accommodate three or four boys. It could be barricaded and made invisible by stacking wood in front of it.

"How long did you hide?" Edith asked, picturing the boys crowded inside the small space.

Eric shrugged. "Two, maybe three hours. The soldiers came back several times." He smiled cunningly. "I guess they didn't believe the cook, and they wanted to surprise us. But we made it to our safe places each time."

Eric made it sound so simple, like playing a game. He could have said, "Oh yes, we just played hide-and-seek," instead of "Oh yes, we just hid from the Nazis." Maybe for Eric and some of the others, avoiding capture and outsmarting the Nazis really was an adventure. But for Edith, fear and uncertainty never went away. Danger was always just around the corner, waiting to get her if she let her guard down. She had to stay watchful and alert. That was the only way she was going to survive.

# CHAPTER 15

## August 1943
## The House Is Closing

Within a few days, almost in spite of herself, Edith settled back into the house routines. With school out for the summer, the days passed peacefully, with a lazy summer energy. There was even a marriage for two of the group leaders. At the wedding dinner, Eric and the other photographers presented the newlyweds with a photo album of pictures taken during the ceremony. It wasn't quite a banquet — rationing and food restrictions saw to that — but the feeling in the house was optimistic, even hopeful. "Perhaps the war is ending," the children whispered. "Maybe our parents will come for us soon."

Edith prayed every night that Mutti would come. And when she visited Gaston, she pretended it would happen for sure. But in her heart, she believed differently. She had been led to think that she would be safe too many times. This time she was not going to be so easily fooled. So, when Shatta and Bouli called an emergency meeting in August 1943 to announce the closing of the house, Edith was not surprised, just very sad.

"Conditions are worsening in France," Shatta began. "It is no longer safe for all of you to be here."

The room pulsed with the reaction. Some children looked shocked and dazed, and sat in stunned silence. Others shouted "No!" and "I want to stay — don't send us away!"

"Are we going camping again?" a boy asked. "Should we pack our things?"

Shatta shook her head sadly. "No. I'm afraid this time five or six days in the woods will not make a difference. We must close the house for good."

"Now that America has joined the fight against Hitler, I'm confident that the war will not last too much longer," said Bouli. "There are positive signs that the Nazis will be defeated. We all know the Nazis surrendered to the Russian armies at Stalingrad. And they have surrendered in North Africa as well. The tide is turning."

"Yes," agreed Shatta. "Things *are* changing. But not soon enough for our house. The French authorities are supplying the Nazis with lists of Jews in this area so they can transport us to the concentration camps. There is increasing danger for the mayor here in Moissac and for all of our friends who have kept our secret. It will be better for them, too, if we leave."

"But where will we go, Shatta?" Sarah was the one who asked the hard questions for all of them. "Who can hide a houseful of Jewish children?"

"We don't have all of the answers yet," replied Shatta with some hesitation. "But over the next few weeks, we will let you know where you will be going and when." She sighed deeply before continuing. "There is no place that can take all of you. You'll be going to homes and boarding schools, two or three together, staying with people who will hide you. I promise you all that I will not leave this house until each and every one of you is in a safe place."

There was that word "safe" again, thought Edith. *Could there really be enough safe places for us all?*

"We can no longer live openly as Jews," Shatta continued. "You will be given new identities — new birthplaces, new names that are not Jewish. You will need to learn these names and answer to them as if you were born with them. All of this will take practice. But I am confident that you will learn these skills, just as you learned camping skills. Remember always that you are Scouts, and Scouts are always prepared." Then Shatta dismissed the group with a tired wave of her hand. Edith could not even begin to understand how frustrated Shatta must have felt that they could not all stay together.

That afternoon, Edith and Sarah went to see Eric in the photography workshop. He was working with several other older children, sorting through papers and documents.

"Look," he said, picking up one of the sheets of paper. "The church has given us blank baptismal certificates. We're going to fill one in for everyone in the house." This document would affirm that Edith and the others had participated in the religious ceremony to initiate them into the Catholic Church.

"Shatta says that we are all getting new names," said Sarah. "I wonder who I'll be."

"What a silly question," said Edith. "You're Sarah. This is a disguise. It's just pretend. It doesn't change who you are."

"If this plan is going to work, it's going to take more than pretending," said Eric. "It's not like you'll be able to jump out from behind your disguise and shout, 'Surprise! I fooled you!' You're going to have to believe in your new identity and believe that you are someone else. Look," Eric said, pointing to the name below his own photograph on one of the identity documents. "I'm Etiènne Giroux now."

Edith didn't like the sound of this. What was it Mutti had said to Edith before leaving her here in Moissac? "Remember who you are." How could she become anyone else?

"I wonder where we'll be sent," Sarah continued. "Or if we can stay together."

Edith hadn't thought about that. Shatta said that they would be sent away in small groups. But Edith had assumed that she would remain with at least a few of her friends. The thought of being alone was even more terrifying.

"Well, I'm not going to be sent anywhere," said Eric.

"What do you mean?" asked Edith. "Everyone is going to a safe home."

"Not me," replied Eric. "I'm leaving. I'm joining the Resistance in the east of France. These papers will get me across the country to fight the Nazis. What do you say to that?"

Edith stared at Eric in disbelief. She knew about the Resistance. She knew that all across Europe, groups of men and women were risking their lives to slow down Hitler and his armies — stealing weapons, blowing up railroad tracks and ammunition supplies, passing information to the Allies. Most of the fighters were Christians, but Jewish men and women were also in the Resistance. And Eric was about to join them.

"Jews are fighting back wherever possible," Eric continued. "Just a couple of months ago, there was a revolt in the Warsaw ghetto. The Jews there refused to be imprisoned any longer. I want to fight back too."

Edith knew about the Warsaw ghetto. Bouli had told them about the revolt there. But thousands of Jewish men, women, and children had been killed in the uprising. Eric seemed to have forgotten that part. But nothing would stop Eric from something he was determined to do. Edith could only wish him good luck.

"When are you leaving, Eric?" she asked softly.

"Soon," he replied. "When these identity papers are done. Don't look so sad. No one has caught me yet. And no one will. Besides, I'm still official photographer, so while you're here, let me take your pictures for the new documents."

Edith and Sarah lined up to pose for their photos. When it was her turn, Edith stared somberly at the camera. She didn't smile but made a silent promise. *No matter what those papers say, I won't forget who I am, Mutti.*

# CHAPTER 16
## Remember Who You Are

Over the next few days, Shatta and Bouli met with groups of children to show them their identity papers and rehearse their new names. Edith stared at her photo on her new document. That was her face staring back at her, unsmiling and serious. But it was the name underneath the picture that held Edith's attention. She was no longer Edith Schwalb. The name beneath her photo was Edith Servant. Edith Servant. She whispered the name several times, rolling the strange sound around her mouth. Edith Servant. Edith Servant. Well, at least she kept her first name. That was some relief. But still, after she'd spent eleven years being one person with one identity, this new name was too strange to grasp fully.

Edith looked over at Sarah. Her face was pale, and she was moving her lips as if she was studying for a test. "Well? What's your name?" asked Edith.

Closing her eyes, Sarah whispered, "Simone. Simone Carpentier."

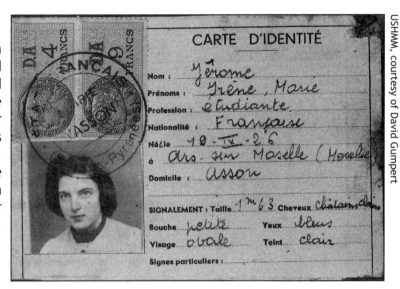

Identification papers issued to a girl named Irene Marie Jerome. Her real name was Inge Joseph. Edith had false identification papers similar to this one.

USHMM, courtesy of David Gumpert

Edith nodded. There was nothing to say. She stared at the cross on her baptismal certificate. Even that looked so out of place beside her name on the paper. Edith Servant was Catholic. Did that mean Edith Schwalb had to give up her Judaism?

"Practice saying your new names," Shatta was saying to the group. "From now on you must stop using your old names and refer to one another only by your new ones." Shatta picked up Sarah's papers. "If I say the name Sarah, you must not answer," she said, looking into Sarah's eyes. "There must be no response in any way — not a turn of the head, not even a nod." Shatta returned the papers and moved on. "Repeat your new names over and over until they seem completely natural. Your safety depends on this. There can be no mistakes, as you will have no second chances.

"On your documents, there is a new place of birth," continued Shatta, as she moved around the room. "Learn the name of the city or town where you were born. Study how it is spelled. Test one another until you can declare your place of birth with ease."

According to her documents, Edith Servant had been born in some place called Enghien-les-Bains. Edith raised her hand, terrified. "Shatta! Where is this? I've never heard of En ... En ..." She gave up trying to pronounce it.

Shatta looked at the paper. "Enghien-les-Bains," she repeated. "It's a city about twenty kilometers south of Paris."

Edith closed her eyes tight so she wouldn't cry. How could she convince anyone that she had come from a city she knew nothing about? What if someone asked her what it looked like? Or what street she had lived on, or what her school was called? What would she say? She was doomed. Enghien-les-Bains. "Bains" meant "baths." Maybe they made bathtubs there. No, that was ridiculous. But inventing a whole life was even more ridiculous.

The meeting was over. Edith took a deep breath. "Come on ... Simone," she said. "Let's go practice."

# CHAPTER 17

## *Leaving Moissac*

Edith stood in the middle of an unfamiliar street surrounded by people she did not know. Angry men glared at her, fists raised. Soldiers pointed guns at her. Strange children were shaking their heads sadly and staring. All of them were shouting the same question, demanding an answer: What is your name?

*My name? My name,* she thought, looking wildly around for someone to help her. Finally, helplessly, she whispered, "Edith. My name is Edith."

"Edith what?" they yelled. "What is your name?"

"It's Edith … Edith …" Oh, what was the name on her papers? Why hadn't she practiced? Now it was too late. She was going to be arrested because she couldn't remember her name. "It's just Edith," she cried.

"Don't you know who you are?" they yelled.

*I know who I am,* she thought wildly. *Mutti, I haven't forgotten. But I don't know my new name!* The people in the crowd shouted and pressed closer, grabbing at her.

Edith sat bolt upright in bed, gasping. Then the shadows in her dormitory began to take on their familiar shapes, and she recognized the sound of her roommates' breathing. The moon shining through the window cast a warm, comforting light. Edith lay back, waiting for her heart to stop pounding.

*This is never going to work*, she thought. *I can't become someone else. I can't pretend all the time and never make a mistake.* So much was being asked of her and the others at such young ages. At eleven, she should have been thinking about parties and playing games, not hiding her identity in a fight for survival. Edith closed her eyes, but she couldn't sleep. She lay squeezing her pillow until the first rays of the morning sun drifted into the room.

❧

As soon as her chores were done, Edith visited Gaston. "You've already had practice at this, Gaston," she reminded him, as they sat together on the front stoop. "Remember when we went camping and you stayed with a family? You pretended to be their son. You called them Maman and Papa. You're good at make-believe."

Gaston seemed quieter and more withdrawn than ever. "Can I come with you when you leave?"

"Shatta and Bouli decide where we will go. You know that, Gaston. If it were up to me, we'd hide together until Mutti came for us. But …"

Gaston looked away. They sat silently until it was time for Edith to leave. She hugged her brother tightly, and promised to see him the next day; but she worried that she might not be able to keep her promise. Already, several boys and girls had left to go into hiding. They left quietly, accompanied by counselors, usually in the night, so no one would notice. No one asked where they had gone. It was best not to know. Their unmade beds in the morning were the only evidence they had ever been there. Even Eric disappeared one night, with several other boys. Edith never had the chance to say goodbye. Each night she looked around the room, wondering who would still be there in the morning. And she wondered when her turn would come.

She didn't have to wait long. One night, she suddenly felt someone shaking her shoulder gently.

"Edith, wake up." She rolled over and looked into the eyes of her choir director. "It's time to go," whispered Henri. "Get dressed quickly and quietly."

Next to her, Sarah was also getting out of bed. Edith had hardly dared to hope that she and Sarah might be going into hiding together. She quickly dressed and grabbed the small suitcase that was packed and lying under her bed. She and Sarah tiptoed out of their room.

Henri and two other girls were waiting for them. They all walked quietly down the stairs and out the door of the house. This time, Edith did not turn back. She didn't want to see the house in this ghostly darkness. She only wanted to remember what it looked like in the daytime, with the sun glistening off the number 18 and the windows full of laughing and chattering children. Briefly Edith wondered if Shatta was looking out after them. Edith had not said goodbye to Shatta, or to Bouli, or to any of the other children.

"No sentimental goodbyes," Shatta had said at their last meeting. "You are all in my heart and we will meet here again, when this war is over."

Perhaps it was for the best. How could she have said goodbye to Shatta and Bouli? How could she thank them for everything they had done for her? They were family. From now on, she would add them to the prayers that she whispered every night for Papa, Mutti, Therese, and Gaston.

# CHAPTER 18

## A New Home

When they arrived at the station, Henri spoke to the girls before boarding the train. "I need to give you information about where you are going." Henri whispered, even though the platform was virtually deserted. "We will be traveling west about one hundred kilometers, to a small town in the Gironde district called Ste-Foy-la-Grande. There, we will go to a boarding school where you will be staying. The director is expecting us. She is the only one who knows who you really are, and knows you are Jewish. And she is the only one who can know."

Henri paused, allowing this information to sink in. One by one, the girls nodded — they all understood. This new town would be different from Moissac in every possible way: no townspeople keeping their secret safe, no mayor warning them of danger.

Henri was interrupted by the arrival of the train. He and the girls boarded a third-class carriage, where they sat facing one another on the wooden benches. Edith glanced around at the passengers. An elderly man and his wife slept halfway down the carriage. The moment the train had left the station, they had drifted off, their heads bouncing in rhythm with the wheels. A young woman several seats away had her nose buried in a book. She didn't look up. Edith wondered if any of these people could tell that she was in disguise.

The conductor passed through the car. "Billets! Tickets," he demanded. The old couple awoke; the young woman put down her book. Henri passed the tickets to the conductor, who glanced briefly at the group and moved on. The old couple settled back into sleep, and the young woman continued reading.

Henri motioned to the girls to move close and listen. "I need to finish telling you this," he said, his eyes darting this way and that, to see if anyone was listening or looking at them. But no one took any notice.

"The girls at the boarding school will be told that a group of orphan children are coming to stay. Your parents have been killed; you have nowhere else to go, so the school has agreed to take you in."

This was the last piece in Edith's identity puzzle. Now her disguise was complete. She had a new name, a new place of birth, and her parents were dead.

"I know you have been practicing for weeks, but I must repeat this. From now on, you must call one another by your new names, even when you are alone. You must try to forget about who you were."

*Never!* Edith thought.

"Now try to rest," said Henri. "We'll have to change trains later, and we won't arrive in Ste-Foy-la-Grande until early evening. I've brought us some bread and cheese."

For the remainder of the journey no one spoke. Strangely, Edith did not feel frightened, just numb. Sarah, sitting quietly next to Edith, seemed equally dazed. Edith looked over at the other two girls. Both were older. One of them she did not know well. The other was Ida, the same girl who had first told Edith and Therese about Moissac. It was a relief to know that they would all be in this boarding school together. There was comfort in that. Suzanne, the oldest, had kept her first name, as Edith had. Ida had become Irene. *Suzanne, Irene, Edith, and Simone.* Edith whispered their names over and over, turning them into a rhyme.

> *Suzanne, Irene, Edith, and Simone,*
> *Four Jewish girls who have no home …*

The silly jingle danced around in Edith's head until they arrived in Ste-Foy-la-Grande.

❧

From a distance, the school was unimpressive, a square, two-storey brick building on a quiet street. It had a small front yard surrounded by a wrought-iron gate. The yard was filled with beautiful ash trees, their delicate green leaves glowing in the dusky light. The school was next to a cemetery, and Edith shuddered at the idea of gravestones for neighbors. The girls followed Henri up the stairs and into the director's office.

"We are taking you in at great risk," the director, Madame Picot, said, as she greeted the children. She was formal in manner, with neither the kind words of Shatta nor the warmth of Bouli. "You must never, I repeat, never, reveal your real names or your religion," she continued. "Your lives will be in jeopardy if you do so, and so will ours. You are Catholic orphans who have come to board with us."

Henri came forward. "We are most appreciative of everything that you are doing," he said. "The children understand the risks you are taking, and they will be careful. Here are their baptism certificates, identity papers, and ration cards," he added, placing the documents in the director's hands.

"There isn't much food," the director replied. "But we'll get what we can." Madame Picot looked over the girls once more. "There are not many who will take Jewish children these days. So I expect you to be grateful for what you are given."

Henri turned back to the Edith and the other girls. "I must go now. But one of us from the house will try to visit you once a month, if we can. Here." He pulled four small, wrapped packets from his pocket. "Chocolate — from the cook, to say goodbye. Look after one another," he said. And with that, he was gone.

Edith looked down at the chocolate, a treasure in these days of rationing. But she would have gladly given it up to be back in Moissac.

"All right, then," Madame Picot said, after Henri had left. "Follow me. You will unpack and meet your roommates."

The girls followed the director up the stairs. She paused at one large room and motioned Ida and Suzanne inside. Then she continued on to the room for Edith and Sarah.

How grimy the room was — so different from Moissac, where everything had been clean and fresh! Here the walls were stained; several shelves were broken, and the wooden floor was cracked and discolored. A stale odor hung in the air. There were at least twenty beds and, at one end of the room, a row of basins. There were tall, dirty windows along one long wall. Edith was relieved that the two empty beds were next to each other. The girls placed their suitcases on them and began to unpack. Edith glanced out the window and shuddered. The room overlooked the cemetery.

"If you're not careful, the ghosts will float up and get you while you're sleeping."

Edith turned to face several girls who were staring at her and Sarah.

"What's your name?" The tallest girl was speaking to her. All of the girls looked older and not particularly friendly. Henri had said that they were mostly farm girls who lived in the house during the week while attending school. On weekends, they returned to their homes in the country. "What's your name?" the girl asked again, louder this time.

"Edith," she replied, and then paused. "Edith Servant." The name tasted strange in her mouth.

"Hello. I'm Simone Carpentier."

Edith wondered where Sarah got such confidence.

The girls stared at Sarah and Edith a little longer, then shrugged and turned away, uninterested.

"Orphans," the tall girl muttered.

Edith didn't have very much to unpack, and it took only a few minutes to stack her things on the small shelf next to her bed. She sank onto her bed. This room looked as abandoned as Edith was feeling. Even with Sarah here, she felt completely alone. She didn't have her parents or siblings to comfort her. She didn't have the people from the house in Moissac to protect her. She no longer even thought about Sophie, or whispered to her when she needed something to hold on to. Edith realized that she had only herself to rely on — herself and whatever memories she could summon.

She gazed out the window, careful not to look at either the cemetery or the hole in her grubby blanket. She was exhausted: tired from the journey and weary from being Edith Servant. And this was only the first day. How would she ever manage in the days and weeks to come?

The first stars were just beginning to peak out, glittering in the dim skies outside her room. A sliver of a moon appeared on the horizon. Edith gazed at the darkening sky. It was Friday night. If she were back in Moissac, Sabbath preparations would be well under way: white tablecloths and candlesticks, chicken soup, and songs performed by the choir.

Edith looked around the room. The girls who hadn't left for the weekend were reading or chatting. Suddenly, she had an idea. She motioned to Sarah, who looked puzzled but followed Edith out of the room and down the hall. Edith signaled for Sarah to wait outside the other dormitory. She emerged a moment later with Ida and Suzanne. The girls tiptoed down the stairs and out the back door into the large yard. They dashed to a small, secluded area away from the house. When they reached this farthest corner of the yard, Edith stopped and faced the others.

"Shabbat shalom," she blurted out. Her eyes sparkled like the stars twinkling above her head. "I wish you peace on this Sabbath."

Sarah gasped, and Ida and Suzanne quickly looked around. Was anyone watching? Could anyone see them? Could anyone overhear what they said?

"Shabbat shalom," Edith repeated. "If we speak quietly, no one will hear us out here."

Sarah hesitated. "Shabbat shalom," she finally whispered.

"Shabbat shalom," said Ida, followed by Suzanne.

Edith grabbed hands with her friends and began to dance in a circle. They sang softly and skipped lightly, mindful of the dormitories close by and the possibility of being seen. They danced slowly at first, and then picked up speed until they were skipping and twirling with a joy they had not felt in a long time. They swung each other around and around, rejoicing in a Jewish dance of celebration. Edith knew that in the morning, she would have to pretend to be someone else; but for this moment, under the stars, in the peace of this Sabbath night, she danced, reclaiming her faith and her freedom.

# CHAPTER 19

## 1943
## Ste-Foy-la-Grande

Life was hard for Edith in the new house. It wasn't that the Jewish girls were treated badly. No one was deliberately cruel. They were simply ignored. It was almost as if they didn't exist. No one showed them either kindness or concern. No one looked after them. And in the absence of caring counselors, and without the nurturing of Shatta and Bouli, Edith found it impossible to look after herself.

Each day, she put on her only dress for school. She could bring so little with her from Moissac: one dress, one skirt, one pair of overalls, a few sets of underwear and socks. Edith and Sarah tried rinsing their clothing in the sink, but soap was scarce, and as the weeks passed, Edith's clothes became filthy and ragged.

Even worse, she herself became dirty. In these grubby surroundings, there was no opportunity to bathe. Over time, as no one cared, Edith stopped caring herself. The only things to look forward to were the visits from Germaine.

Henri had promised that someone from Moissac would visit the girls and supply new ration cards each month. The first time

Edith (seated right) was sent to the school in Ste-Foy-la-Grande along with Ida (back left), Suzanne (back second from right), and Sarah (seated left).

Germaine arrived, Edith nearly jumped into her arms. Germaine brought the girls a small piece of chocolate and an armload of compassion.

"The first thing I'm going to do," she said, "is take the four of you to the bathhouse." The girls followed Germaine through the town, past the little row of restaurants, the bookstore, and the church. No one paid any attention, even though they must have looked like street urchins.

In the bathhouse, Germaine gave the girls small pieces of soap. The warm water was heaven on Edith's young body. She threw back her head, opened her mouth, and let the water run over her, washing away a month's dirt and grime, sorrow and loneliness. If only she could go back with Germaine — back to the warmth of Moissac. There, she had felt protected and cared for.

Edith longed to ask Germaine a million questions: Had she seen Gaston? Where had Eric gone? Was he safe? What about Shatta and Bouli? Yet she sensed that knowing the answers might jeopardize the safety of those she loved. So, Edith said nothing, but cherished the time with Germaine and was saddened each time they had to say goodbye.

Germaine's visits helped, but one bath a month wasn't enough to keep the dirt and bugs away. At first, when Edith and Sarah scratched at their scalps, they thought their unwashed hair was making them itchy. But they couldn't ignore the evidence: they had lice.

The farm girls paid little attention to the bugs. They kept their hair cropped short or treated their scalps with kerosene to kill the pests. Edith and Sarah tried the kerosene treatment, too. It helped Edith, but not Sarah.

"The itching is driving me crazy," she complained early one morning as she and Edith sat by the stove in their classroom on the ground floor. Their dormitory was bitterly cold now that November was upon them, and there was little heat elsewhere in the house.

"You have to stop scratching, Sarah," said Edith. "Look what you're doing to your head!" Sarah's scalp was raw from the scratching. Ugly red welts stood out amid her once beautiful long hair.

"I can't help it," said Sarah, sitting on her hands. "It feels like they're eating through my skull!" She scratched some more, pulled a tiny bug from under her fingernail, and examined it carefully.

"How can something so small be so disgusting?" she asked, flicking the bug onto the stove. For a moment, it lay there, then sputtered and danced up and down. Finally, it exploded right in front of Sarah and Edith. The girls looked at each other, amazed, then burst out laughing.

"That's it!" cried Sarah. "We'll blow them up! Goodbye, lice!"

She and Edith began pulling lice from Sarah's hair, flicking all they could find onto the hot stove. One after another, the bugs sizzled and popped. It was both crazy and fun.

"Take that, you awful bug!" shouted Edith. "That'll teach you to come near me!" Usually so wary and gentle, she felt wild and strong. And that was a very good feeling. She and Sarah exploded lice until they heard the teacher and students approaching. Then they jumped into their seats, lowered their heads, and tried to look inconspicuous. Their moment of fun was over.

But as amusing as that moment had been, it didn't solve the problem of Sarah's lice. She continued to scrape and claw at her scalp. She tried to stop. She tried to ignore the terrible itching. She tried wearing gloves, day and night, to keep her from clawing at her scalp; but the lice continued to nest, the scratching went on, and the welts grew more inflamed and painful. If the scrapes were not going to become infected, there was only one solution.

"No," wailed Sarah. "I won't cut my hair. Anything but that!" She grabbed the strands of her hair and pulled them into a tight bun at the back of her head, trying to hide her hair in her fist. Edith stood in front of her, holding the classroom scissors. She didn't say anything; she just stood, firmly looking at her friend. Finally, Sarah gave in and sat down in front of Edith.

Wordlessly, Edith began to cut. Sarah winced each time the scissors sliced through her hair. But she didn't cry and she didn't complain. The hair kept falling, almost like tears themselves, cascading in a puddle around her feet.

In the days that followed, Sarah became quiet and withdrawn, as if her spirit had been cut off with her hair. Her eyes grew sadder and more hollow, and her stare more vacant.

"Sarah, please don't be so sad," begged Edith, trying to give back some of the hope her friend had always given her. "Your hair will grow back, you'll see." Sarah didn't respond. Besides, Edith knew that it wasn't just losing her beautiful hair that made Sarah so sad. It was losing everything in her life – her family, her freedom, her identity.

Edith tried to cheer Sarah by appearing lighthearted; but deep inside she was as sad as Sarah. Hiding like this was so much harder than hiding in Moissac or in the woods during Camp Volant. Here, Edith had to hide who she was. She knew there was no way to pull Sarah out of her despair and didn't have the energy to keep trying. Besides, lice and dirt seemed minor problems compared with hiding your identity — and starving.

Edith was always hungry. Rationing had become so severe that some days all she had to eat was a bowl of porridge for breakfast and soup with one piece of potato for lunch. Dinner was a disgusting mush of creamed leeks, a creation so vile that Edith's stomach lurched at the smell. She could see the bones on her chest. She could feel her ribs sticking out. It didn't help that the farm girls made jokes about the bad food and rationing in the cities and competed in their descriptions of the fresh produce, meat, and cheese that awaited them at home on the weekends. Edith and Sarah could only listen and dream of food.

"When I go home, I'm going to have a huge bowl of stew, with mountains of mashed potatoes, and ice cream and fruit tarte and ..."

Edith and Sarah were walking in the yard one Sunday morning. Here, out of earshot of the house, they could talk without fear of saying something that might give them away as Jews.

Sarah nodded and smiled faintly. "I just want to go home."

"I know, but I can't help talking about food." Edith was trying to ignore Sarah's gloom. "Maybe I'll have a croissant — maybe ten — or a huge bag of sweets."

The girls knew this yard well. It was here, in the far corner that they danced every Friday night, wishing Suzanne and Ida another peaceful Sabbath. But now their attention was drawn in the other direction, toward the kitchen. The cook was dumping something into a large bin. She scraped and shook her pot, then turned and walked into the building.

"Come on," said Edith. "Let's see what's over there." She maneuvered Sarah toward the garbage bin. The girls looked around carefully, making sure no one could see them, then peered inside. The smell was overwhelming — a combination of rotting vegetables and decaying meat. But amid the decomposing waste, Edith spotted something.

"Hey," Edith said. "I think there's some food in there."

"Let's just go." Sarah peered fearfully about. "We'll get into trouble."

"It'll just take a second."

Edith plugged her nose, reached into the garbage, and pulled out a bunch of rotting carrots.

Then the two girls ran toward the outhouses in the yard. Safely inside, Edith examined her find, carefully cleaning away the muck and breaking off the bits of carrot that were too moldy to eat.

"It's not farm food, but it's better than nothing." Edith grinned.

She handed half her prize to Sarah, who smiled gratefully. The girls sat down to eat. *The cook was sloppy to throw away food that can be eaten,* thought Edith. If the director had known, she would have been furious. But the cook's carelessness proved Edith and Sarah's salvation. Rotting carrots had never tasted so good. It wasn't a feast, but it filled some of the empty corners of Edith's stomach. The girls finished eating just as the church bells began ringing. They had lost all track of time.

They ran into the house just as the director was coming out of her office. "Where have you been?" she demanded.

"Just for a walk in the yard, madame," Edith replied, breathing hard.

Madame Picot eyed the girls suspiciously. "Well, join the others," she said finally. "It's time for church."

Edith and Sarah fell into line behind the director, and marched off toward the church.

# CHAPTER 20
## Prayers to God

When the girls were told that they would have to attend weekly church services, Edith was terrified. It was one thing to *tell* people she was Catholic, but how could she *act* Catholic. Others would expect her to know the rituals of the Church, and the Latin service. Surely someone would notice her ignorance, and her real identity would be revealed.

But she had no choice. She watched the girls around her and copied every movement — kneeling when they kneeled, folding her hands in front of her, bowing her head, and crossing herself in perfect rhythm. She learned the appropriate French responses, and muttered an inaudible chant when Latin was required. Before long, the charade became familiar and easy.

The grandeur of the church in Ste-Foy-la-Grande never ceased to amaze Edith. It was an enormous, gray stone building with two high steeples and a large cross above the door. The rich dark wood of the pews shone; and the sun filtered through the colorful stained-glass windows high above, casting bright, multicolored light the length of the aisles. The statue of the Virgin Mary seemed to smile down at Edith, reaching out as if to offer the protection and caring that she longed for. There may have been a war raging, but here, in this place of worship, there was only peace and serenity.

Edith walked confidently to the rows of pews and bowed her head. She slid across the pew next to Sarah and knelt on the narrow kneeler in front of her. Then she made the sign of the cross, just as she had watched the others do. With the first two fingers of her right hand, she touched her forehead, the middle of her chest, then her left then right shoulder. Finally, she folded her hands and closed her eyes.

*God, you don't mind, that I'm pretending to be Catholic, do you?* Edith asked silently. She knew that God was God, no matter where you were or how you prayed. The God in the church was the same God that she knew, and she prayed under her breath.

"Keep Mutti and Papa safe. Watch over Gaston and Therese, and all the children of Moissac. Look after Shatta, Bouli, and Germaine and Henri. Sarah is so sad. Please protect her and help her smile again. And, God," she whispered, "I'm trying to be brave, but I'm really scared to be here. Please help me, too."

Edith opened her eyes and gazed at the statue of the Virgin Mary — at her gentle eyes and outstretched arms. She had a sudden urge to throw herself into those mothering arms. The priest was chanting and the congregation responded, reminding Edith of the synagogue services she had attended so many years ago in Vienna.

She had not understood the rabbi's Hebrew words any more than the priest's Latin, but then as now she enjoyed the simple chants.

All too quickly, the service was over. The congregation rose and Edith followed. They crossed themselves, and she did the same. Suddenly, next to her, Sarah gasped and Edith froze. The two girls locked eyes, realizing at exactly the same moment that Edith had crossed herself with her left hand instead of her right.

Edith's face went red with the pounding of her heart, and sweat broke out on her brow. Making the sign of the cross was so basic that to cross yourself incorrectly in a Catholic church was almost like telling the whole world that you were an imposter. Shatta's voice rushed into her mind: "There can be no mistakes. Your safety will depend on this."

Not only had Edith jeopardized her own life, but she might have placed Sarah and the others in danger as well. She desperately searched the faces of the people around her. Had anyone noticed? Men and women were shaking hands and greeting one another, wishing each other peace and a rapid end to the war.

No one had paid her any attention.

Sarah reached out a hand to her friend and the two girls quickly walked out of the church.

"That was close," Edith whispered.

Sarah nodded. "I thought Jeanette next to me saw, but it doesn't look like it." Like all the girls, Jeanette was giggling and talking with her friends, ignoring Edith and Sarah as usual. For once, Edith was grateful that she and Sarah were nearly invisible. Being invisible meant that mistakes might go unnoticed. Still, they would have to be extra careful.

Edith worried for the rest of the day. *Maybe I should just not leave the school,* she thought. *Maybe I should stay inside, avoid places where one small lapse might give me away.*

So, it was with mixed feelings that Edith followed Madame Picot and the others out the door the next day for a routine trip to the department store in town. There, madame would buy supplies for the school — and the girls would carry the packages. Edith often wondered what became of all those purchases. She and her friends from Moissac certainly never saw the soap or clothing that madame bought.

Edith walked slowly up and down the half-empty aisles of the store, inspecting the sparse items on the shelves and filling the empty spaces with thoughts of all the things she'd like to buy. Before long, she was lost in childhood memories of playing "store" with Therese.

*"I will take a bottle of perfume, and two bars of soap. Oh no, not that perfume — the very expensive one."*

*Therese, the shopkeeper, quickly rushed to get the things her young customer had requested. "Of course, mademoiselle, the very best."*

*"Then I'll take two bottles. Please wrap them up."*

As the memory of those playful days swept back over her, Edith reached out to touch the colorful ribbons displayed on a table. She longed to have just one to tie in her hair, just as Mutti had done so many times. She was so lost in her happy daydream that she did not notice someone stopping directly in front of her.

"Hello, little girl."

Startled, Edith looked up into the face of a Nazi soldier.

"I said hello," the soldier repeated.

"Bonjour. Good day," Edith murmured. The words practically stuck in her throat.

The soldier looked at her with a slight smirk. He was tall and straight, arms folded easily across his chest. She could hear the squeak of his tall black boots as he swayed slightly back and forth.

"What's your name?" The soldier leaned closer. Edith could smell his cigarette smoke.

"I'm Edith," she finally croaked. "Edith Servant."

"Edith," he said thoughtfully, looking her up and down. "A German name, yes?"

Edith's head was spinning. What did he mean? Did he hear something in her accent that didn't sound French? Had he guessed she was Jewish? Would he drag her away? Shoot her? All of these thoughts raced through Edith's mind as she faced this Nazi soldier. Then, suddenly, she knew what to say.

"Edith is a French name." Edith replied, staring the soldier squarely in the eye. "Haven't you heard of Edith Piaf?" Edith Piaf was France's most beloved singer. Her picture appeared in magazines and newspapers, and everyone knew her music.

The soldier paused a moment and then chuckled. "Yes, of course. Very clever, little sparrow, just like Edith Piaf." He tapped her lightly on the head and moved on.

Edith closed her eyes tightly, trying to control her shaking. Surely the soldier must have sensed that she was Jewish but had chosen to ignore it. Perhaps her quick thinking had amused him. It had certainly saved her life.

"Are you all right?" Edith opened her eyes to see Sarah staring at her.

"Did you see what just happened?" Edith asked.

Sarah nodded.

That was twice that she had come close to being discovered, Edith thought, as she followed Sarah and the others out the door and back to their school. That added up to two very scary experiences. It was more than she could handle in two days. It was more than most people could manage in a lifetime.

# CHAPTER 21

## April 1944
## Sarah's Sadness

For several days, Edith could not get the soldier out of her mind. She could still hear the creak of his boots, and smell the odor of stale cigarette smoke. Her dreams were filled with soldiers shouting questions at her as she crossed herself over and over with her left hand.

Edith would awake confused and disoriented. *Where am I?* she wondered, lying in the dark. *Who am I?* she'd ask as she sat in school. *Did I tell the man delivering milk that my parents are dead? Where am I from? Where was I born?* And all the while, Mutti's last words haunted Edith. "Remember who you are." *Who am I*, Edith mused, *when every day I lie to the people around me?*

It was weeks before the pain of that day faded to a dull ache. Edith pushed it deep inside her, where others couldn't see how much it hurt. That was the only way she knew to keep going. It was the first warm day in spring. Edith and Sarah had been at the school for seven months. How was it possible? Would they spend another winter in hiding?

The girls were sitting on the school steps, listening to bombs exploding in the distance, like irregular muted thunder. One explosion, silence, then two louder blasts. These bomb blasts had become a regular occurrence.

"Maybe the bombing's a good thing," said Sarah cautiously. "Maybe it means the war will be over soon."

Edith nodded. She knew that the Allied airplanes were closing in on Hitler's armies.

Several nights earlier, she and Sarah had been scrounging for food behind the kitchen and she had heard the voice of President Franklin Delano Roosevelt of the United States of America talking on the radio.

*"Until the victory that is now assured is won, the United States will persevere in its efforts to rescue the victims of brutality of the Nazis. This government will use all means at its command to aid the escape of all intended victims of the Nazis."*

The president's message was spoken in English, a language that Edith was learning here at the school. She did not understand every word that she heard, but some of them were clear. The president in his commanding authority had said, *"the victory that is now assured."* That meant that he was confident that the United States and the Allies would defeat Hitler and his armies.

"We have to hope it's true," Edith now said.

Above their heads, the leaves of the ash trees whispered and swished in the warm breeze. Edith turned her face up to the sun.

Among the dark green leaves she could see hundreds of butterflies, their wings tightly closed, clinging to the leaves and swaying in the gentle wind. As she watched, they began to flutter, opening and closing their bright orange wings streaked with bold black and white stripes. Then, the whole mass lifted and flew off, like a bouquet of flowers carried by the wind.

Edith was so entranced that she barely noticed Sarah jump up and run toward a young man standing by the open gate. She looked over just as Sarah flung herself into his arms.

"Jacques!" Sarah cried. "What are you doing here? How did you get here? Edith, this is my brother, Jacques." Sarah was so excited that she was babbling.

Jacques was tall and thin, his clothes ragged and ill fitting. Nervously he pulled off his cap and glanced around. "I've been traveling for weeks, Sarah," he muttered, "looking everywhere for you. I finally found Germaine, your counselor in Moissac. It took some doing to convince her I was your brother and that she could tell me where you were." Jacques smiled wryly. "I don't think she liked the looks of me."

Sarah was practically dancing. "The important thing is, you're here." Then she looked around and lowered her voice. "But you can't stay, Jacques. The others think we're orphans, with no one. Oh, but please, tell me how you are, and how are Maman and —"

"I don't have much time, Sarah," Jacques interrupted. "And there's no kind way to tell you. Maman has died. A cough in her chest. I tried to find a doctor, medicine, but no one could help us."

Jacques and Sarah's mother had been hiding in a barn — the farmers let them stay as long as they didn't make trouble. He described how Sarah's mother had grown weaker and weaker, until she had no fight left. He had buried her in the farmer's field before heading out to look for Sarah. As Jacques spoke, Edith could see Sarah shrink back into her shell.

"And Papa?" Sarah whispered.

Jacques shook his head. "Still no word."

"What about you, Jacques?" Sarah asked. "What are you going to do?"

"I'm going to join the Resistance. With Maman gone, I'm free to go."

Sarah shook her head. "Free?"

Jacques shrugged. "Free enough."

He stayed a few more minutes. Then he hugged Sarah, said goodbye to Edith, and walked down the path and out the gate.

The two girls sat together on the front steps, saying little. A butterfly flitted past Edith's face and then soared high up into the clear blue sky. Moments earlier the sky had been filled with these delicate butterflies. Now there was nothing.

*This is so cruel*, Edith thought. She had seen the butterflies come to life just when Jacques had arrived to announce the death of Sarah's mother. Life beginning and life ending. Edith placed her arm around Sarah's shoulders and sat with her friend until it was time to go inside to class.

# CHAPTER 22

## The Bombings

Sarah barely said a word for the rest of the day, and Edith didn't even try to talk to her. What was there to say? Besides, all Edith could think about was her own mother.

Was she being selfish, she wondered, to be preoccupied with her own family when Sarah was living her nightmare? But she couldn't help the thoughts that filled her mind. Was Mutti safe? Was she lying sick somewhere, fighting to stay alive? Would Therese be next to appear on the steps of the school with terrible news? That was unimaginable. But who could have envisioned everything that had already happened in the past months and years? It was all unthinkable.

After classes that day, Edith sat on Sarah's bed, holding her hand. Sarah lay, quiet and pale, her eyes closed. At first, Edith barely noticed the muted sound of engines in the distance, and the dull explosions. But the drone of airplanes quickly became louder.

"That's strange," said Edith. "It sounds like the planes are flying this way. Maybe they're going to circle back to their targets."

But the hum became a rumble and the rumble a roar, until it seemed as if the planes were headed right for the school.

Edith's grip on Sarah's hand tightened. "Sarah," she said urgently. "I think we'd better —"

The explosion shattered the window above the bed. Edith and Sarah dove to the floor, clutching each other tightly and covering their heads. The floor heaved, tossing Edith and Sarah against each other and then, against the bed frame. A sharp whistle pierced the air.

"Another one's coming!" screamed Edith.

The next bomb exploded in the graveyard next door. The detonation reverberated inside Edith's head as the lights in the room flickered and went out. Pictures fell, along with chunks of plaster from the ceiling. Smoke and dust filled the room. Shards of glass bounced around the floor with each vibration. Edith could hear the other girls screaming and crying in terror.

She could not breathe. Her heart pounded so loud that it seemed louder than the planes. Surely the next bomb would hit their building. *Is this how it will all end?* Edith wondered. *No!* her mind screamed. *This can't be. I won't die like this. I won't.*

Seconds later the whistle began again, and Edith closed her eyes. But this time, the bomb blast was farther away. The explosion rocked the room gently one more time. She heard the planes rumble off into the distance, growing fainter and more muffled, and then there was quiet.

Many minutes passed as she and Sarah lay under the bed, holding each other and trembling in shocked silence. There were no sounds around them. As loud as the bombs had been minutes earlier, now the silence was equally deafening. And then, slowly, Edith raised her head. "Sarah, are you all right?"

Sarah lay face down, totally still, one arm covering her head. Finally, she looked over at Edith.

"I'm fine," she whispered.

Cautiously, the girls crawled out from under the bed, shaking off the dust and fragments of glass. The room was a shambles. Mattresses, pillows, and clothing had been flung in all directions. Splintered shelves lay amid piles of glass and plaster. Edith and Sarah gingerly stepped around the debris.

A moment later, Madame Picot ran into the room. "Is everyone all right? Anybody hurt?" Her face and dress were covered in dust.

Seeing that except for a few bruises and small cuts, everyone was fine, she took a deep breath. "Well, that was quite an adventure. Just a few broken shelves and windows. Nothing that can't be repaired." Madame Picot spoke calmly, but Edith could see the slight trembling of her hands. "So, now we must clean up. Move the beds back into place," she continued. "Carefully sweep up the glass. I want this room back in order immediately."

# CHAPTER 23

May 1944
Another Move

Slowly but surely, the girls began to move in response to the director's instructions. Several pushed the beds back into place and shook the glass fragments from blankets and pillows. Others gathered clothing and carefully picked up the larger pieces of glass. Edith reached for a broom and began to sweep. The smell of smoke and dust filled the room and burned her eyes. She moved close to the window for fresher air and looked outside. People were running with buckets and hoses to fight a fire in a nearby building. The ground outside her window was smoking, giving off a haze that made the graveyard look even more eerie than usual

It was comforting to put things back in their places. Cleaning up the mess was like wiping out the events of the day. By making the room tidy, you could pretend that nothing bad had happened. But you couldn't really wipe out the war.

Over the next days and weeks, the bombings continued all around Ste-Foy-la-Grande, filling Edith with both hope and terror. The planes meant that the war might end soon, Hitler might be defeated, and Edith's life might return to normal. But at the same time, she was terrified that the bombs might kill her first.

Wouldn't that be ironic, Edith thought wryly, to have come this far, only to be blown up by those coming to rescue you. She longed to scream up at the planes, "We're Jewish girls hiding here. Don't hurt us!" And after each attack, Edith could breathe easily once more. She could hope again that the war would soon be over. And that she would still be alive.

The bombers' goal was to destroy the nearby railway bridges. Without the railway, soldiers, goods, and ammunition could not be moved efficiently and Hitler's armies would be isolated, cut off from reinforcements and supplies.

As the bridges around Ste-Foy-la-Grande were regularly bombed, the danger for everyone in town increased. So, it was no surprise when the announcement came that the school was to close and that the girls would be moved once more.

It was Germaine who brought the news. "I'll be moving you immediately," she announced brusquely when she had gathered Edith, Sarah, Ida, and Suzanne together. Most of the other girls had already left the house for their farms and homes; the school was practically deserted. "We've located homes for each of you. Edith, you will come with me now. I'll be back for the rest of you tomorrow."

"Isn't Sarah coming, too?" Edith blurted out. "Aren't we staying together?"

Germaine shook her head. "Each family can take only one girl. We're lucky to have found anyone willing to do that. You'll have to say goodbye for now." Germaine stood to end the meeting. "Pack quickly, Edith, and meet me at the front door. We don't have much time, and I have many things to do."

Left alone, Edith and Sarah sat silently, hands clutched tightly.

"Do you think we'll see each other again?" Sarah finally asked in a voice so small that Edith had to lean forward to hear.

"Of course," Edith replied, although both knew that the confidence in her voice was false. "You can't give up, Sarah. We've come too far. You must stay strong." Those were Mutti's words. Now Edith was passing the same message on to Sarah.

"I'll try to remember," Sarah replied, and they hugged each other fiercely.

# CHAPTER 24

## Marianne's Room

It was less than a two-hour walk to the farm on the outskirts of Ste-Foy-la-Grande. The farmhouse was nestled between two small hills next to a quick-flowing stream. There was a wooden barn next to the house and a large enclosed pasture. In it, four cows were drinking at a trough. As Edith and Germaine approached the house, Monsieur and Madame Merleau opened the door and invited their guests in.

"We know all about you," Monsieur Merleau said, as they all sat down to a dinner of grilled fish, potatoes, and fresh bread. It was the kind of feast that Edith and Sarah had dreamed about. Edith took a slice of crusty bread, smothered it in jam, and shoved it quickly into her mouth.

"You poor child," Madame Merleau said. "You are thinner than my scrawniest chicken. But I'll put some fat on you."

Madame Merleau had the kindest face Edith had seen in a long time. Her hands were rough and hard from years of farm work, but her eyes were gentle. "It's a crime what's happened to the Jews," she added, pouring Edith a tall glass of milk. "Especially you children."

"But we will not speak again about you being Jewish," Monsieur Merleau said, in his deep soothing voice, "as it increases the risk to all of us. We are happy to have you here with us. We will keep your secret safe."

"We are only doing what all decent people should do," his wife added.

"You must call me Oncle Albert, and my wife Tante Marie," Monsieur Merleau said. "You will meet your new cousin, our daughter, Marianne, and her fiancé soon. We have told our neighbors that a niece may be coming to stay, so —"

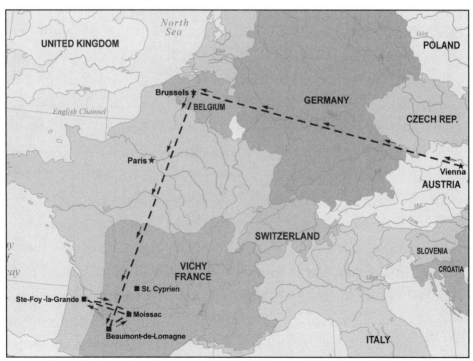

Edith's journey from Austria to Belgium and through France

"It's enough, Albert," Madame Merleau interrupted. "Look at the child. Her face is falling onto her plate. She needs sleep."

"Yes, please, Madame … er … Tante Marie." All the fear that Edith had held inside for so long seemed to seep away, leaving her worn out. And in the warmth of the Merleaus' welcome she could barely keep her eyes open.

"Come, child. A good scrub, and then I'm putting you to bed." Tante Marie looked sternly at her husband. "Any more explaining can wait until tomorrow. Now, Albert, please walk mademoiselle back to the road. We need you out of the kitchen."

A large pot of water was heating on the stove. Tante Marie took Edith's filthy clothes and dropped them into the woodstove, then scrubbed her from head to toe, washing away the grime and dirt. Edith dried herself in front of the stove, gratefully accepted a clean nightgown, and followed Tante Marie to a cozy bedroom at the back of the house. An elderly woman in a long, flowing dress, holding a young child, seemed to smile at Edith from a photograph. A chest of drawers stood against one wall of the room, a small bed along another.

Tante Marie picked up Edith's suitcase. "I'm going to get rid of these clothes. I'll give you some dresses that Marianne has outgrown. They'll fit you fine. Nothing fancy, just simple and clean clothes." She stroked Edith's forehead. "I hope you will be happy here, my dear. Good night. Sleep well."

But Edith lay awake a long time, watching the shadows grow longer and darker across the walls. Before Moissac, she had shared a bedroom with Therese. Since then, Sarah had always been in the bed next to her. Edith suddenly felt very alone. She longed for the sound of someone else's breathing beside her. For the first time in months, she wished she still had her doll, Sophie. Edith's arms ached to wrap themselves around Sophie's soft body, and to bury her face in the doll's hair and clothing.

But there was something far worse than this sudden feeling of loneliness. There was a small hole in the window shutter across from Edith's bed, through which moonlight trickled into the room. And in the darkness and solitude of this unfamiliar place, her mind began to race. *A soldier is going to come into the field, shoot through that hole, and the bullet will kill me,* Edith thought wildly. She shifted, first to the left, then to the right, but she was still directly in line with the hole. She was doomed no matter where she lay.

"Breathe," Edith commanded herself, speaking out loud in the dark room. The sound of her voice almost echoed in the emptiness. "Breathe deeply." She forced her body to relax, her shoulders to soften, and her breathing to return to normal. Then she thought of Mutti, as she had so many times when she was afraid. In her heart, she still believed that Mutti was safe. "I'm waiting for you, Mutti," Edith whispered into the darkness. This is what always kept her going. The belief that she and Mutti would soon be reunited is what gave her strength. And that thought enabled her to close her eyes and sleep.

# CHAPTER 25

## June 1944

It didn't take long for Edith to adjust to the farm routine. She awoke each day at dawn to milk the cows and release them into the pasture to graze. Then she cleaned out their stalls and headed in to help with breakfast. Edith attacked her tasks with energy and enthusiasm. The warm spring sun brought color to her cheeks, and she could feel her arms and legs becoming stronger.

True to her word, Tante Marie gradually fattened Edith up. As her stomach was able to tolerate more food, she was plied with meat and potatoes, and butter on her bread. Rationing was strict elsewhere, but not on the farm. Gone were the days of sneaking food scraps out of the garbage.

Marianne Merleau was a big girl with a wide bright smile and a thick braid that bounced and swayed down her back It reminded Edith of Sarah's beautiful hair before the lice. Marianne's fiancé, Martin, brought sweets for Edith whenever he visited — which was almost every day. He followed Marianne around like a puppy, beaming with pleasure at each smile she sent his way. Their obvious affection for each other made Edith blush and giggle.

One sunny day, when Edith had been at the farm for several weeks, she, Marianne, and Martin decided to go for a picnic in a field upstream of the house. They spread a blanket among wildflowers — red, purple, and yellow anemones, which Mutti so loved, daisies and white lilies. Bees circled lazily; their gentle buzzing mingled with the chirping and whistling of robins and sparrows.

Martin pulled out his clarinet and started to play. Edith lay back on the blanket and let the sun and the music seep into her body. Half asleep, she floated in time, memories and images drifting through her mind. One moment she was walking with Papa in Vienna, clutching her father's arm on a day just like this one. The image faded, and Edith was standing on the steps of the house in Moissac. Mutti was walking away as Edith called desperately after her. Another moment passed. Now Edith was dancing joyfully in the yard of the school in Ste-Foy-la-Grande. Stars were sparkling in the sky as she wished Sarah a peaceful Sabbath. With the final image of her bedroom at the farm, Edith slept.

She dreamed she was alone with the bees droning lazily above her. The buzzing grew louder as more bees circled her head, then louder still. Edith opened her eyes and sat up with a start. That buzzing sound was all too familiar — airplanes! And they were coming closer.

She looked around wildly. They were in an open field. There was nowhere to take cover. "Bombers!" she shouted. "We have to hide."

Marianne threw her arms around Edith, struggling to control her trembling. "Edith, it's okay. You're safe with us. They're Allied planes. They won't hurt us."

Marianne was wrong. The Allies had bombed Ste-Foy-la-Grande. They had to run! But Marianne held Edith tightly. The roaring was deafening now; it pounded Edith's brain and reverberated through her body. She buried her face in Marianne's shoulder.

"Open your eyes, Edith!" Marianne shouted. "Look!"

Cautiously, Edith opened her eyes a crack. There were at least ten planes flying low in formation. Then she saw what Marianne was trying to show her.

Martin was jumping up and down, waving at the planes. As Edith watched, the lead plane dipped one wing, as if waving back. Edith raised her arms above her head and laughed. Now she knew she was safe.

She watched until the last plane disappeared over the horizon. Then she asked, "What day is it today? I want to remember this."

Marianne thought a moment. "It's June 6."

Edith sank down once more onto the blanket. "Mutti's birthday," she said in amazement. Martin picked up his clarinet and played a silly rendition of "Happy Birthday." This was a sign, thought Edith. The Allies are here, she sang over and over in her head. The war will soon be over. Mutti will come for me.

# CHAPTER 26
## The Reunion

Edith didn't even know it at the time, but June 6, 1944, marked an event far more important than Mutti's birthday. On that day, more than a hundred thousand Allied ground troops in thousands of boats attacked along the coast of Normandy, in northwest France. The invasion took the German High Command by surprise, and Nazi forces across Europe began to retreat. World War II did not officially end until May 1945, but by September 1944, the war was over in France.

Edith remained on the farm throughout the summer of 1944. During that time with the Merleau family, she was happy and well taken care of. Most important, she was safe. Then, in September, Germaine arrived to take her back to Moissac.

"Shatta and Bouli have returned to the house," Germaine said. "We are trying to bring back all the children as well."

Edith said a tearful goodbye to Tante Marie, Oncle Albert, Marianne, and Martin. They had become family at a time when she had so desperately needed their nurturing and care.

The house in Moissac looked unchanged; but everything felt different. Edith was twelve now, and had had a lifetime of experience, good and bad, since she had been there last.

"Hello, my dear." Shatta and Bouli came out to greet Edith and gave her warm hug.

"We're so happy you've returned safely," said Bouli.

"Go inside," continued Shatta. "Get settled and we'll talk later."

A group of unfamiliar counselors were checking off children's names as they arrived. "What is your name?" one asked, flipping through the lists of names.

"Edith Serv … No, wait." Edith paused. "Schwalb. I'm Edith Schwalb. That's who I am," she declared. In that moment, she reclaimed her name and the identity that she had been forced to hide.

"Schwalb," the counselor repeated. "We have another Schwalb. There he is." Gaston was standing behind Edith, smiling shyly.

"Gaston!" screamed Edith. She twirled him in a circle, hugging him and shouting his name over and over. Finally, she stepped back to look at him. Gaston had grown much taller, but he was painfully thin and his eyes looked sadder than she remembered. She could not even begin to imagine what his life had been like. Perhaps, in the months to come, she and Gaston would be able to sit together and share their stories. Perhaps they could begin to understand what the war had done to each of them. But that would wait. For now, all that mattered was that he had survived.

Over the next few weeks, all the children who had lived in the house in Moissac trickled back, every one alive and safe. They were joyfully reunited, but their eyes held the painful truth of what they had been through.

Edith hadn't dared to hope that she would ever see Sarah again; but one morning, Sarah appeared at the dormitory door.

Edith hugged her friend tightly. "Your hair has grown back," she said finally.

Sarah nodded, reaching up self-consciously to touch her head. She was still so quiet. It would take a long time for her to break out of her shell — to begin to talk and share her story. The end of the war had brought freedom for everyone. But there were still some, like Sarah, who remained imprisoned in sadness and despair. All Edith could do was to be there for her friend — a shoulder to cry on and a compassionate listening ear.

One day in late September, Edith was sitting on the front steps. The early signs of fall were everywhere. Leaves were beginning to turn yellow, and the air had a freshness that heralded cooler weather. But the flowers in the field were still in full bloom, and the birds flew overhead.

People were walking by on the streets of Moissac, going about their business almost as if the war hadn't happened: mothers walked hand in hand with their children; shopkeepers tended their stores; cars had reappeared on the streets.

In the distance, Edith could see two women carrying small suitcases striding up the road toward the house. At the end of the walkway, they turned up the path to the front steps.

Edith looked hard at the taller woman. She recognized that walk, knew that face!

She flew off the steps and into Mutti's arms.

A plaque in Moissac dedicated to Shatta and Bouli Simon for the work they did protecting Jewish children during the war.

# EPILOGUE — NEW BEGINNINGS

*1945*

*Moissac*

"Look, it hasn't changed at all!"

Once again, Edith and Gaston were in front of the three-storey gray stone house in Moissac. The number 18 still gleamed in the morning light. The window shutters, with their crisscross designs, were flung open to let the sunlight shine through the windows, just as it used to. Across the road, a cool breeze drifted in from the river. Edith took a deep breath, thinking back over the year that had passed since the war had ended.

Her reunion with Mutti and Therese had been the happiest moment of her life. Together with Gaston, they returned to live in a small apartment in Beaumont-de-Lomagne. Edith went back to the local school, even further behind in her studies. Still, her life was happy, complete except for one piece — Papa.

For weeks, Edith and her family begged for news of him from the trickle of Jews returning from the concentration camps. She stared at these people, haunted and wasted-looking, and she felt guilty. How could she have complained about her conditions in Ste-Foy-la-Grande when these prisoners had suffered so much? She turned away from their skeletal bodies and prayed that among those returning, someone would bring news of her father. Then, one day, one of Edith's cousins walked into the apartment. He had been imprisoned along with Papa, and brought the news that the family had been dreading.

After their arrests, he said, he and Papa had been taken to the concentration camp at Auschwitz. American soldiers liberating the camp at the end of the war generously overfed the prisoners. After years of being starved, Papa was one of many prisoners whose bodies could not handle the food, and he died the next day.

Edith was shattered by the news. She had held on to the hope that her father would return to his family, to her. But now he was gone, and all Edith had was the memory of this strong and loving man.

At the news, Mutti seemed to grow old in front of Edith's eyes. This strong, beautiful woman, who had fought so hard to protect her family throughout the war, was worn out and disheartened; and as time passed, Edith could see that caring for three children was too much for Mutti. She had no fight left.

Then, Edith came up with a perfect idea. "Please, Mutti, let me go back to Moissac." It was so simple, Edith thought. She would go to live in the house in Moissac. After all, it felt like her real home, not Beaumont-de-Lomagne or anywhere else in France. There, in the house, she would not be a burden. She was fourteen now — she could help look after other children, like the young counselors who cared for her during the war. She had thought it all through. She would take Gaston; Therese would remain to look after Mutti.

Mutti refused. She had just brought her family back together. How could she have them separated again? But Edith was persistent, promising to visit Mutti whenever she could, just as Mutti had promised to visit Edith in Moissac. She begged and pleaded, and in the end, Mutti realized that this was the best decision. It made sense for Edith and Gaston to return to Moissac.

So Edith now stood with Gaston by her side, staring up at the house that was home. "Come on," she said, squeezing her brother's hand. "Let's find Shatta."

Edith and Gaston entered the house, walked across the hallway, and paused at the office door. She knocked softly.

"Entrez! Come in," a voice called.

Edith peered inside. There was Shatta, seated behind her big wooden desk. She took one look at Edith and leapt to her feet. "Edith!" she cried. "How wonderful! And Gaston! Look how much you've grown!" Gaston squirmed in Shatta's embrace but was clearly happy to see her and happy to be here. "How long will you stay?" Shatta asked. "You know you are welcome."

Edith took a deep breath. *This is the third time I have come to this house*, she thought. The first time, she had been unwilling, terrified to be separated from Mutti. The second time, as the war was ending, she had come with Germaine, still uncertain about the future. This time, Edith felt strong. She had chosen to come to Moissac, chosen to come home.

"I'll stay as long as I am needed, as long as I can help."

Edith remained in Moissac until 1949. She was then asked to go to Paris where she became a counselor in a new home, looking after orphaned Jewish children. It was there in 1953 that Edith married Jacques Gelbard, who also worked in this house. Two years later, Edith and Jacques left France for Canada. A year after Edith arrived, she brought Mutti to live with her in Canada and cared for her until her mother's death years later. Today, Edith lives in Toronto, surrounded by four sons and nine grandchildren. Gaston became a famous chef in Toronto, who once ran for mayor of the city. The Gelbard family has now been active in the Scouting movement for three generations — a tribute to the organization that enabled Edith to survive the war.

Edith in 1949.

Many years after the war — Gaston in his restaurant kitchen.

Edith (bottom left) and girls from the house in Moissac after the war. They are wearing scouting uniforms and are on a camping trip.

Edith (seated far right) as a counselor, with children from the home in Paris in 1950.

Edith (top right) and more children from the home in Paris in 1950.

Above: Edith's wedding to Jacques. Pictured also are Therese (far left), Gaston (seated below Therese), Edith's mother (far right), and other young relatives.

Right: Edith and Jacques Gelbard in Paris, 1950.

In May 2004, Edith visted Moissac and Ste-Foy-la-Grande.

Edith in front of the house in Moissac.

Edith in front of the gates to the school in Ste-Foy-la-Grande.

Edith in Ste-Foy-la-Grande. The school where she lived is on the right. The cemetery is to the left behind the tall hedge.

# AUTHOR'S NOTE

*Hiding Edith* is a true story. Edith Schwalb was born in Vienna, Austria, in 1932. She and her family left Austria as World War II approached and eventually made their way to southern France. After her father was arrested by the Nazis, her mother and sister went into hiding in the countryside; Edith and her brother, Gaston, were sent to the house in Moissac.

The house was funded by the Jewish Scouts of France (Éclaireurs Israélites de France) and run by a young couple, Shatta and Bouli Simon. Henri Milstein was the choir director, Germaine Goldflus one of the counselors. Sarah Kupfer became Edith's close friend. For four years, Shatta and Bouli harbored Jewish children whose parents had gone into hiding or had been arrested by the Nazis. Of the more than five hundred Jewish children who lived in the house during the war, only one did not survive: her parents took her away, against the advice of Shatta and Bouli. The family was caught and deported to a concentration camp.

The entire town of Moissac knew about the house and its purpose, and the children were welcome in the local school. The townspeople never betrayed the Jews living among them. If there were the threat of a Nazi raid, the mayor would send word to Shatta and Bouli. The children would go camping in the hills around Moissac and return when the danger had passed.

In writing *Hiding Edith*, I have tried to stay true to Edith's life as a hidden child. In some cases, she was not able to recall the names of people she had encountered during the war, so I invented names for several people. As well, Eric Goldfarb and Edith never met in Moissac, though they were there at the same time. Eric was sixteen years old and stayed for six months before joining the Resistance. Eric and Edith did meet, in Toronto, many years after the war.

In May 2004, many of the children of Moissac, including Edith, together with the children and grandchildren of Shatta and Bouli returned to the house for a ceremony of remembrance. Two plaques were unveiled: one honored Shatta and Bouli Simon; the

A plaque placed in Moissac in 1950 by the child survivors of the house. It says in part, "To the citizens of Moissac who protected, helped, and saved hundreds of young Jewish children during the dark years of the German occupation."

other honored the former mayor and the citizens of Moissac who, at the risk of their lives, collectively saved the lives of hundreds of Jewish children.

May 2004 — A gathering of child survivors and citizens of Moissac in front of the house. Edith is standing close to the center in a white jacket. There are also young scouts from the community standing in the foreground.

# DEDICATION

*To Edith Schwalb Gelbard, a courageous and admirable woman*
*For Gabi and Jake, with love as always*

❧

# ACKNOWLEDGEMENTS

First and foremost, my thanks and gratitude to Edith Gelbard for sharing her story with me. The first time I heard Edith talk about her experiences in Moissac, she was speaking to a group of students. She summarized her story in about five minutes. And in that short time, I heard something remarkable, and knew I wanted to hear more. Edith has patiently endured my thousands of questions with grace and humility, and has always maintained her endearing smile and warm hospitality.

Through Edith, I was introduced to Eric Goldfarb and had the pleasure of interviewing him to fill in some of the missing pieces of this story. Sadly, Eric passed away only a few weeks after our meeting. He was a charming, warm, and witty man and I am grateful we had the opportunity to talk. I am also indebted to his wife, Fée, for generously sharing Eric's photographs and stories.

My thanks, as always, to Margie Wolfe of Second Story Press, for continuing to encourage and embrace my writing. The Holocaust Remembrance Series, of which this book is a part, is Margie's creation. She is a tireless advocate of Holocaust literature for young readers, and I admire and respect her greatly.

Thanks as well to Charis Wahl for her patience and diligence in the editing process. Thanks to Carolyn Wood, Melissa Kaita, Phuong Truong, and Leah Sandals, the women of Second Story. They are a dedicated and talented group and it is a pleasure to work with all of them. I am grateful to the Ontario Arts Council for its support.

I have a fabulous circle of friends and family. To those I see, speak to, or email on a regular basis, to those whom I have come to know within the writing community, and to those who feed me on Friday nights, I love and thank you all.

Every day in my life I have my husband, Ian Epstein, and my children, Gabi and Jake. They nurture my soul, and give me balance, perspective, humor, and love.